THE
NEW YORK PUBLIC LIBRARY
AMAZING SPACE
A Book of Answers for Kids

Ann-Jeanette Campbell

Illustrated by
Jessica Wolk-Stanley

A Stonesong Press Book

John Wiley & Sons, Inc.
New York • Chichester • Brisbane • Toronto • Singapore • Weinheim

To Kerry Acker, *thanks*, and to Stephanie Hutter, *thanks.*
—*A. J. C.*

Copyright © 1997 by The New York Public Library and The Stonesong Press, Inc.
Illustrations copyright © 1997 by The Stonesong Press, Inc.
Published by John Wiley & Sons, Inc.

Library of Congress Cataloging-in-Publication Data

Campbell, Ann.
   The New York Public Library Amazing Space : a book of answers for kids /
Ann-Jeanette Campbell; illustrated by Jessica Wolk-Stanley
      p. cm. — (New York Public Library answer books for kids series; 1)
   "A Stonesong Press book"
   Includes bibliographical references and index.
   ISBN 0-471-14498-3 (paper)
   1. Astronomy—Miscellanea.   2. Outer space—Miscellanea.
 I. Title. II. Series
   QB52.C28   1997
   520—dc21   96-29785
                                                            CIP

10 9 8 7 6

CONTENTS

INTRODUCTION

Space has been described as the final frontier. Where did it come from? How do stars, planets, and comets come into existence, live, and die? How big is the universe? What is it made of? Who, what, where, when, how, and why do we fly into space?

Questions like these bring millions of people to the New York Public Library—and other libraries across the country—every day. Now you can have the answers at your fingertips.

In **The New York Public Library Amazing Space**, you will find the answers to some of the most commonly asked questions about how the universe began, what exists in it, how to locate stars in the sky, what the planets are like, and much more. The easy question/answer format allows you to look up one question at a time or read a whole chapter at once. You'll also find fascinating stories about pulsars, supernovae, sunspots, meteor showers, and black holes. And, following the simple instructions outlined here, you can conduct your own astronomical experiments.

The New York Public Library Amazing Space doesn't tell you everything—we don't know everything—but within these pages are the basics of astronomy: the launch pad from which you can begin to explore space.

The New York Public Library and other libraries all over the country have shelves full of books as well as computers filled with facts to help you learn about space—and any other subject that interests you. It is our hope that this book will encourage you to investigate the libraries in your own town. Perhaps you'll find that your questions don't yet have answers. In that case, you must piece together clues from the information available and leave the rest up to your own powers of scientific thought. Maybe your answer can be used in a future edition of this book!

What is astronomy?

Astronomy is the study of matter and processes that exist primarily beyond Earth's atmosphere. It covers the whole universe—the heavens, the celestial sphere—from microscopic atoms to the vast cosmos. Astronomers study the heavenly or **celestial bodies** such as planets, stars, **comets**, **galaxies**, nebulae, and intergalactic material to determine how they formed, how they exist and function, how they interact, and what may happen to them.

It is important to remember that, as a part of the universe, Earth and its processes are included in astronomy. In fact, Earth is our laboratory. Everything we know about the universe comes first from what we know about Earth and what we can see, perceive, or imagine from Earth.

How did astronomy begin?

Before the invention of the telescope in the early seventeenth century, astronomy was based on observations made by the naked eye. First, people mapped the positions of stars and planets in the sky. Most cultures had their own systems for mapping the sky, but astronomy as we know it today has its roots in classical Greek theories.

In A.D. 150, the Greek astronomer and mathematician Claudius Ptolemy wrote an important treatise on astronomy. In it, he listed forty-eight groups of stars called **constellations**, with names—such as Orion and Perseus—

taken mostly from mythology. In the same way that we can imagine shapes of familiar objects when we look at clouds, so Ptolemy saw traditional figures in groupings of stars.

Ptolemy also noted that the stars seemed to move across the sky. He said that all celestial bodies revolved around Earth, which stood still in the center of the universe. This was the accepted scientific theory for centuries. Ptolemy's view of the universe is called a **geocentric model**, because Earth (*geo* refers to Earth) stands at its center (*centric* means center).

When was it discovered that Earth rotated around the Sun?

The acceptance of this fact was a long time coming. In 1543, the Polish astronomer Nicolaus Copernicus published *De Revolutionibus*, which stated that the planets revolved around the Sun. His theories, however, disagreed with the teachings of the Roman Catholic Church, and the church was the most powerful social and political organization of the time. Ideas such as the **heliocentric model** (Sun-centered model) of the universe were considered heresy, punishable by death. So, while some other astronomers accepted Copernicus's model, they were understandably afraid to admit it.

In 1632, Galileo Galilei, one of the most brilliant astronomers of all time, finally published a book defending Copernicus's view. The Roman Catholic Church brought Galileo to trial for heresy and the astronomer was given the choice to take back what he said or die. Galileo recanted, but the church was powerless to stop the heliocentric model from becoming commonly accepted. (In 1992, the Roman Catholic Church officially agreed with Galileo and Copernicus.)

How did early astronomers distinguish one star from another?

Besides mapping the locations of stars in the sky, astronomers also determined which stars were brighter than others. The Greek astronomer Hipparchus, a predecessor of Ptolemy, first classified stars according to their brightness. He listed six categories of brightness by magnitude. (Magnitude defines how bright the stars *appear* to be from Earth. A star's magnitude is determined largely by how far away from Earth it is.) Hipparchus labeled twenty stars as the first magnitude, or the brightest. The faintest stars, those that are barely visible to the naked eye, he labeled the sixth magnitude.

Galileo Galilei

Galileo Galilei seemed to be larger than life. Born in Pisa, Italy, in 1564—at the culmination of the Renaissance—Galileo was not just the first person to focus a telescope on the stars; he also turned the view of the world upside down.

Galileo was a master of astronomy, mathematics, physics, philosophy, and publicity. His image (and probably the reality) was that of a temperamental genius: brilliant and witty, but also caustic and nasty. Prominent people sought his company—until he took up the unpopular and dangerous task of defending Copernicus's sun-centered view of the solar system in his published works.

We accept as fact that the Sun is the center of the solar system. Imagine, however, knowing *just as surely* that Earth is the center. We might have said: "*Everyone* knows that the Sun revolves around the Earth. Only a few crazy scientists think otherwise."

In 1543, Nicolaus Copernicus had published his treatise proposing that all the planets, including Earth, revolved around the Sun. This breakthrough was welcomed by a few, but only in private, for the most powerful government in Europe at that time—the Roman Catholic Church—had a vested interest in the status quo. Its whole system of beliefs—and its authority—rested on Earth being central to the universe.

Galileo's public support of the Copernican worldview upset the church. Its leaders had dealt with other heretics by ignoring them or burning them at the stake. But the church could not ignore Galileo.

In 1634, Galileo was brought before the church courts and told to recant his heretical beliefs about the solar system. Faced with the alternative, torture and death, Galileo finally gave in. According to legend, as he left the courtroom, Galileo claimed—under his breath—that regardless of what he was forced to say, Earth still moved around the Sun.

Galileo was under house arrest for the remainder of his life, until 1642. The church officially accepted the Copernican model of the solar system 350 years later, in 1992.

When was the telescope invented?

At the beginning of the seventeenth century, Hans Lippershey, a Dutch eyeglass maker, discovered that when he looked through two lined-up lenses at different ends of a long tube, distant objects appeared closer and larger. He was probably not the only one to make this discovery, but his name has come down through history.

How did the astronomical telescope develop?

Galileo built many telescopes, each more powerful than the last, and in 1609 he was the first to use the instrument—called "Galileo's ladder"—to study the sky. The great astronomer Sir Isaac Newton modified Galileo's telescope by using mirrors instead of lenses. A musician and amateur astronomer named William Herschel, who discovered the planet Uranus in 1781, recognized that the bigger the mirrors were, the more powerful the instrument would be.

In the twentieth century, telescope technology has exploded, but the basic idea that bigger is better still guides its development. The most recent radical improvement in viewing space through telescopes is our ability to send telescopes beyond Earth's atmosphere and record images we could never hope to see from our planet.

In 1789, William Herschel unveiled a telescope that was 40 feet (12 m) long, with a 2,000-pound (900-kg) metal mirror measuring 48 inches (120 cm) in diameter; this allowed him to look further into space than anyone before him.

What do optical telescopes do?

Most of what we know about the universe comes from the study of light from space objects. The general purpose of a telescope is to gather light from objects in the sky, making them larger, brighter, and clearer so that we can study them in detail.

Two major types of optical telescopes are used to view space. The **refracting telescope** uses lenses. The **reflecting telescope** has mirrors instead of lenses.

How does a simple refracting telescope work?

Let's say we are looking at the Moon through a refracting telescope. Light from the Moon is gathered by the **objective lens**, which sits at the open end of the telescope. As the light enters the lens, it is bent just as light

World's Largest Refracting Telescopes

Observatory	Location	Aperture: inches/feet/meters
Yerkes	Williams Bay, Wisconsin	40/3.30/1.01
Lick	Mount Hamilton, California	35/2.90/0.89
Paris	Meudon, France	33/2.75/0.83
Potsdam	Potsdam, Germany	31/2.58/0.80

bends when it goes through water or a prism. The light bends again as it leaves the far side of the lens, coming together again at the **focal point** of the telescope, appearing larger and brighter than it does to the naked eye. A lens, called an eyepiece, is attached to the end of the telescope and allows you to view and magnify the image.

How does a reflecting telescope work?

A reflecting telescope uses mirrors, whereas a refracting telescope uses lenses. Light gathered into a reflecting telescope first travels the length of the telescope's tube until it reaches a mirror placed at the tube's end. The light bounces off that mirror, called the **primary mirror**, and journeys back along the tube to a point where it refocuses into a reflection of the original image. The point where the light refocuses is called the **prime focus**. Photographic or computer graphic equipment can be placed at the prime focus to record the image, or another mirror, called the **secondary mirror**, can be used to reflect the image into an eyepiece for viewing.

World's Largest Reflecting Telescopes

Observatory	Location	Aperture: inches/feet/meters
W. M. Keck*	Mauna Kea, Hawaii	387/32.35/9.82
Special Astrophysical	Mount Pastukhov, Russia	236/19.60/6.00
Palomar	Palomar, California	200/16.60/5.08
Mount Hopkins	Amado, Arizona	177/14.75/4.50

*At least two other larger telescopes are under construction at the Keck Observatory.

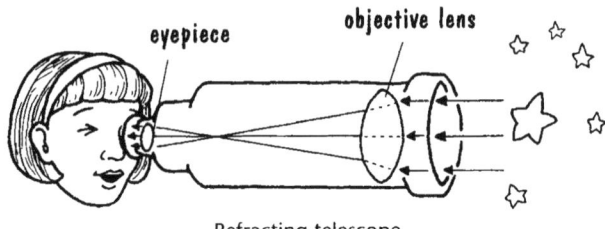

Refracting telescope

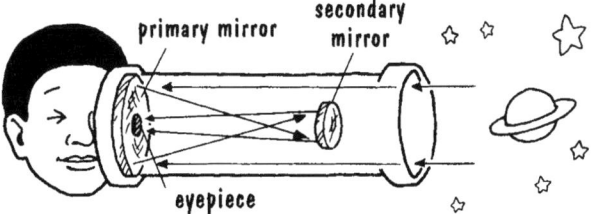

Cassegrain reflecting telescope

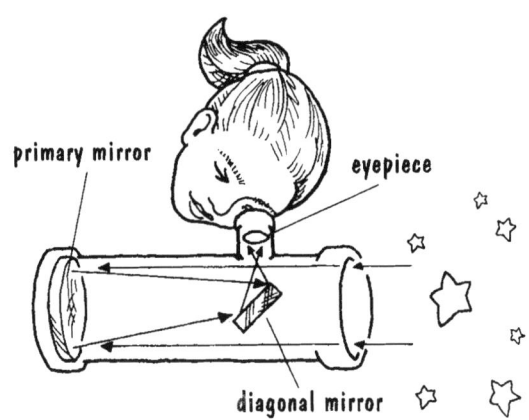

Newtonian reflecting telescope

Two kinds of secondary mirrors are used in reflecting telescopes. A Newtonian reflecting telescope, invented by Sir Isaac Newton, uses a flat, angled mirror to steer the light directly through an eyepiece. The **Cassegrain telescope**, named for a contemporary of Newton, uses a curved, concave mirror instead of a flat, angled mirror. Incoming light is reflected off the primary mirror, onto the concave mirror, back toward the primary mirror, and out through a minute hole in the primary mirror that holds an eyepiece. Changing the curve of the secondary mirror alters the distance the light has to travel in the telescope, which changes the size and clarity of the image. A whole set of mirrors with different amounts of curvature can be used interchangeably in a single telescope.

What determines the power of an optical telescope?

The size of the objective lens in a refracting telescope, or the primary mirror in a reflecting telescope, and the distance the light travels through the telescope's tube are the most important elements in determining the power of the telescope.

The diameter of a lens or mirror is called the **aperture**; the larger the aperture, the more light can be gathered and focused. The distance between the center of the lens or mirror and the point where the object's light rays are bent to a common point is called the **focal distance** or focal length. In both kinds of telescopes, the size of the image grows larger when focal distance is longer.

How do astronomers measure really big distances?

Everyone relies on numbers to express distance, but when distances are immense, too many digits have to be used to make sense. For example, the distance between Los Angeles and New York is 14,710,080 feet, or 2,786 miles (5,280 feet = 1 mile).

We don't have to use as many digits in miles as in feet. To express distance in space, astronomers most commonly use measures called astronomical units, light-years, and parsecs.

What is an astronomical unit?

The **astronomical unit (AU)** measures the relatively short distances within our **solar system**. One AU is the mean distance from Earth to the Sun, about 93 million miles. We can say that Pluto's average distance from the sun is 40 AUs rather than saying it is 3.72 billion miles.

The world's largest refracting telescope, at Yerkes Observatory in Williams Bay, Wisconsin, has a lens with a 40-inch (1-m) diameter.

One of the world's largest reflecting telescopes, the Keck II Telescope on Mauna Kea in Hawaii, has a primary mirror that measures 387 inches (9.8 m) in diameter.

The units of light-years and parsecs take care of the even greater distances beyond the border of our solar system.

What is a light-year?

Perhaps the most common measure of space is the **light-year (lt-yr)**. Strangely enough, a light-year can measure both time and space. (Many people believe that time and space are inseparable, simply two sides of the same coin.)

It takes time for light to travel. Light's unvarying speed in space is about 186,000 miles (297,600 km) per second. That's 5,800,000,000,000 (5.8 trillion) miles (9.28 trillion km) per year. So, a light-year, or the distance light travels in a year, is about 5.8 trillion miles (9.28 trillion km).

In light-years, the distance between the star Alpha Centauri and the Sun is about 4.2, which is much easier than saying 23,780,000,000,000 miles, though it means the same thing.

Since the light from Alpha Centauri takes 4.2 years to reach Earth, we are looking at light that is 4.2 years old. We won't be able to see the light Alpha Centauri is emitting today until the year 2001.

What is a parsec?

A **parsec (pc)** is a measure of incredibly large astronomical distance. The word comes from the phrase *parallax second*. **Parallax** means the change in a star's relative position in the sky when viewed from different places, and *second* refers to the smallest measurement of the change (stars move in arcs measured in seconds).

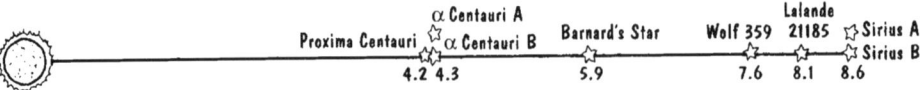

Within 10 light-years of the Sun, there are eight other stars.

Newton's Laws of Gravity and Motion

Much of astronomy deals with the physical laws of motion and **gravity**, which Sir Isaac Newton described in the seventeenth century.

Newton's laws of motion are: (1) Every body of matter remains at rest until it is moved by an external force; (2) when an external force compels an object to move, that object will move in the same direction as the force and at the same rate; (3) an object acted upon externally will react by exerting an equal force on the external force in the opposite direction. You can easily test these laws by playing a game of marbles or croquet.

Newton's laws of gravity are: (1) Every particle exerts a force of attraction on every other particle; (2) the power of attraction is based on the mass of each particle and the distance between them. This power of attraction is gravity, though we really don't know how or why gravity works. When an apple falls from a tree, the particles in the apple and in Earth attract each other. The bigger the object, the greater the force, so the apple falls to Earth. Theoretically, Earth responds to the apple's gravitational pull by rising ever so slightly to meet it.

Motion and gravity always interact. How they do so depends on a given object's power of motion and its size. For example, the Sun's gravitational pull is greater than Earth's because the star is so much bigger than the planet. However, Earth does not crash into the Sun because it is in motion. It travels fast

enough—and is far enough away—to counter the Sun's pull, but not fast enough—or far enough away—to escape it.

Imagine Earth is a baseball and the Sun is the ground on which you stand. Throw the baseball. The ground's gravity pulls the ball to the ground. If you throw the ball faster, it travels farther before the ground's gravity overpowers it. If the ball (Earth) traveled at 383 miles (612 km) per second, it would never hit the ground (the Sun), but go into orbit. Thrown faster than that, the ball (Earth) would be moving fast enough to escape the ground's (Sun's) gravity completely and sail off into space. (Earth's average orbital speed is 18.5 miles [29.8 km] per second.)

Scale of the Universe

Earth to Sun	93 million miles
Sun to closest star, Alpha Centauri	4.2 light-years
Sun to center of Milky Way Galaxy	25,000–30,000 light-years
Diameter of Milky Way Galaxy	100,000 light-years
Milky Way Galaxy to Maffei 1, the farthest galaxy in the Local Group	3.3 million light-years
Diameter of Maffei 1	100,000 light-years
Closest galaxies to Milky Way Galaxy:	
Small Magellanic Cloud	196,000 light-years
Large Magellanic Cloud	210,000 light-years
Outer galaxies:	
Andromeda Galaxy	2.2 million light-years
Whirlpool Galaxy	37 million light-years
Cartwheel Galaxy	500 million light-years
Farthest identified galaxies	>10,000 million light-years
Farthest visible objects (galaxies, quasars)	15,000 million to 20,000 million light-years
Estimated diameter of the universe	15 billion light-years

Imagine a clock with a sweeping second hand. Pretend that you are on Earth at the center of the clock looking up at a star at exactly 12:00. Twenty-four hours later, you look up to see the star, but it appears to have moved to a position that is one second after 12:00. (In fact, it is Earth that moves along its orbital path; the star only appears to move.)

What you see as a movement of one second, however, is actually a vast distance, but you are so far away from the star, the distance appears tiny. One parsec equals 3.26 light-years, or the distance light travels in 3.26 years (approximately 19 trillion miles/30.4 trillion km). Alpha Centauri, the star nearest the Sun, is about 1.3 parsecs away.

What is the electromagnetic spectrum?

The **electromagnetic spectrum** is the scientific name for all of the kinds of known radiation. From shortest (highest frequency) to longest (lowest frequency) wavelengths, they are: **gamma rays**, **X rays**, **ultraviolet rays**, visible **light rays**, infrared rays, and **radio waves** (which include microwaves, television and FM radio waves, shortwaves, and AM radio waves).

Electromagnetic waves surround us every second, but visible light is the only radiation we can see.

What is radiation?

Radiation is energy emitted by a source such as a planet, star, or your own body. We measure radiation in **wavelengths**. Radiation travels in rising and falling motions called waves, like waves in the ocean. Wavelengths are measured from the tip of one wave to the tip of the next. Our eyes can register light waves, which are relatively short, but wavelengths of other kinds of radiation are too short or too long for us to be able to see them.

Radiation waves can also be measured by frequency, or how many waves pass a point within a certain amount of time. Imagine you are standing in the ocean with a stopwatch. You time the waves, counting how many pass you within one minute. If three waves go by, the wave frequency is 3 cycles per minute.

Radiation is usually counted in cycles per second (cps): 1 kilohertz (kHz) = 1,000 cps, and 1 megahertz (mHz) = 1 million cps.

Can an object emit more than one kind of radiation?

Objects usually emit more than one kind of radiation simultaneously. For instance, the Sun radiates everything from gamma rays to radio waves. People emit radio waves, but we can't detect those waves without the proper receiving equipment. (You'd have to use a radio telescope to do so, but all the other radio waves bouncing around Earth's surface would get in the way.)

Scientists believe that some animals see types of radiation other than light. Snakes and bumblebees may see ultraviolet radiation, and bats may see infrared radiation.

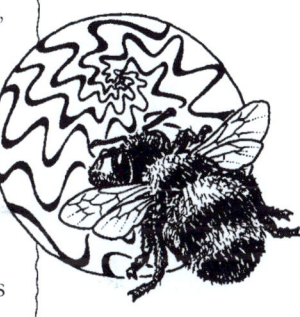

Waves and Rays

All radiation travels outward from its source in a wavelike pattern. The term *ray* is commonly used to describe the rapid, short waves of the upper part of the electromagnetic spectrum: gamma rays, X rays, ultraviolet rays, light rays, and infrared rays. A ray is the straight line along which the waves travel. Slower radiation, with long wavelengths—radio waves—is generally referred to as traveling in waves, not rays. *Ray* implies speed and high frequency—viewed with the naked eye, very fast waves would blur into a line—whereas the word *wave* suggests a slower, more obvious oscillating movement. All in all, however, rays and waves amount to pretty much the same thing: radiation emission.

Technology now allows astronomers to study radiation across the whole electromagnetic spectrum. Research into all the different kinds of radiation provides far more information—and raises many more questions—about the universe than studying light alone.

Is radiation always dangerous?

Some radiation from elements can be deadly. The bombs that the United States dropped on Hiroshima and Nagasaki, Japan, at the end of World War II, were hydrogen and plutonium bombs, respectively. The radiation from other elements is harmless. Seventy-eight percent of the air we breathe is nitrogen, whose radiation obviously is not dangerous.

What is light?

Light is a familiar everyday phenomena that we take for granted. When the Sun or other stars shine, we see light. When we turn on a lamp, we see light. Technically, light is an energy disturbance in the air. Oscillating electric and magnetic fields radiate energy in waves. The wavelengths and frequency fall in the middle of the electromagnetic spectrum, between ultraviolet and infrared rays. It so happens that our eyes detect radiation at those wavelengths and frequencies in the form of light.

Different elements, and the combinations of elements that make up molecules, emit radiation in different ranges of the electromagnetic spectrum. Nitgrogen-based ammonia, for example, tends to emit microwaves. We cannot see ammonia in space with an optical telescope,

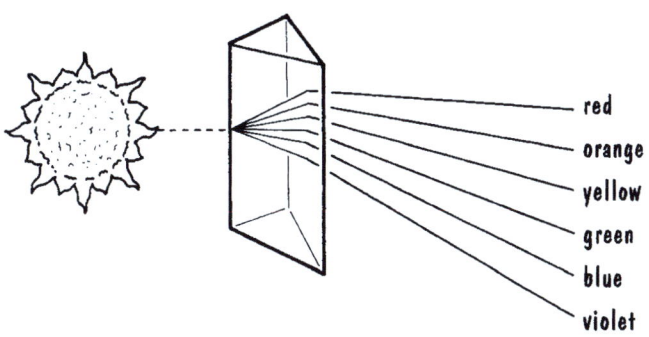

but it can be found using a special microwave telescope. Neon radiation, however, is detected as light. Think of all the neon signs in all the store and restaurant windows you've seen.

Is light white?

We often refer to so-called pure light as white, but light comes in a variety of colors depending on the length and speed, or frequency, of its waves. When light travels through a prism—a solid, multisided chunk of glass—it is separated into its various colors, known as the spectrum. This separation occurs because the wavelengths bend at different angles. From the shortest, fastest (or highest energy) wavelengths to the longest and slowest (or lowest energy), light separates into violet, blue, green, yellow, orange, and red.

The Colors of Light

You have probably seen a rainbow, or light separating into colors through a cut-glass window. You can make your own color spectrum reflect on a wall or ceiling this way:

Lean a mirror against the far end of a shallow pan filled with water (the whole mirror does not have to be underwater). Position the pan so that sunlight—or bright starlight—hits the submerged mirror. Adjust the mirror until you throw a "rainbow" of color against a nearby surface (for example, a wall or ceiling). You will see the clear light become violet, blue, green, yellow, orange, and red, in that order.

Do radio waves have anything to do with radios?

They certainly do. People cannot see radio waves without re-creating them in a visual format—such as by electronically digitalizing the waves in a computer, which

Radio astronomists study low-frequency electromagnetic waves, called radio waves, emitted by relatively cool objects in space. Radio wave detectors are placed in deserts or high in mountains, away from interference from radio waves emitted on Earth—such as those that carry sound to your Walkman. To deliver the latest hit to your ears, radio stations imprint sound on the same kind of radio waves used in astronomy.

in turn displays a "map" of the waves—but we can hear them. We can receive sound carried on radio waves by using a radio receiver, or radio, for short. Radio stations broadcast either AM or FM signals, which stand for amplitude modulation and frequency modulation, two different methods of imprinting radio waves with sound.

What is radio astronomy?

Astronomers who gather information about space by collecting and studying radio waves practice radio astronomy. Radio waves travel from celestial matter through interstellar dust and clouds, so astronomers can identify objects hidden from view. Some objects emit little or no visible light, but radio astronomers help locate them using radio telescopes.

Radio waves can be detected during the day as well as night, since sunlight will not diminish them. Radio astronomers can also study matter in space we never even knew was there because it is invisible to the eye.

Do telescopes record radio waves?

The word "telescope" generally refers to an optical telescope, but instruments designed to collect radio waves are called radio telescopes or **radio dishes**. A radio interferometer is a series of linked radio dishes.

What do microwaves have to do with astronomy?

Microwaves are not only found in ovens. In 1964, scientists Arno Penzias and Robert Wilson recorded microwaves emanating from every direction in the universe. Penzias and Wilson determined that their source was probably the entire universe.

The waves came from everywhere. The only source that can be considered everywhere at once is the universe, if the theory of the big bang holds true. Microwaves would have initiated at the time of the big bang. Since the big bang created all existing matter, everything would radiate the microwaves.

The temperature of the big bang may have been over 500 billion degrees. The microwaves would have cooled a certain amount over the succeeding 10 to 20 billion years. Penzias and Wilson found that their microwaves were just the right temperature to have come from the original blast. Their discovery helped secure the big bang scenario as the prominent theory of creation.

What are infrared rays and how do astronomers detect them?

Infrared rays are long, heat-intensive wavelengths that we cannot see. Telescopes outfitted with heat-sensitive reflectors, instead of mirrors or lenses, gather infrared rays, which are reproduced visually by special photographic equipment. The infrared image of an object is similar to what you see if you put your hand against a

The largest infrared telescope in the world sits on top of Mauna Kea, an extinct volcano in Hawaii.

Einstein: It's All Relative

While Isaac Newton's laws of motion and gravity still have validity as a working model for basic astronomy, physicists rely on Albert Einstein's complex relativity theories in their advanced work.

In Einstein's "special" theory of relativity, an event doesn't necessarily occur at the same time for all those involved; simultaneity is relative, as Isaac and Albert show us.

A bolt of lightning hits the front of the first car of a three-car train and the back of the last car of the train. Isaac, who is standing by the railroad tracks, sees the lightning strike the front and back cars simultaneously as the train's middle car passes him. Albert sits on top of the train's middle car with an angled mirror that allows him to see both the front and back cars at the same time. He sees the front car get hit by the lightning first, and then the back car.

Both Isaac and Albert are in the middle of the train when the lightning strikes. Both know that the speed of light is constant. But Isaac saw that the lightning struck simultaneously, whereas Albert saw it hit at different times. The point of the experiment is that while the speed of light remains constant, time moves more slowly for an observer in motion (Albert) than for an observer at rest (Isaac).

This theory goes on to say that a speeding object gets shorter in length and gains mass as it accelerates toward the speed of light. If an object traveled at the speed of light, which is theoretically impossible, it would shrink to nothing in length, have incalculable mass, and its time would stand still.

Einstein's "general" theory of relativity dealt with the "principle of equivalence," or the idea that gravitational force (a function of space) and acceleration (a function of time) are, in fact, indistinguishable from each other. They can't be separated; they are equivalents. We'll call it "spacetime."

Isaac and Albert blindfold each other and get on an "up" escalator in a local subway station to test this theory. They discover that they can't tell whether they are being pulled by the acceleration of the escalator or by a force of gravity attracting them. (Remember, gravity is not always a downward fall, as we usually experience it here on Earth.)

Now, imagine starlight traveling (great acceleration) near a large planet (great gravitational force). The light bends as a result of gravity/ acceleration, or "spacetime." Not only are space and time one concept; "spacetime" is curved.

If all this baffles you, don't worry. It can take a light-year of "spacetime" to figure out Einstein's theories. And not everyone agrees with them.

very cold window. An outline of your hand appears as a result of the condensation of the warm air from your hand meeting the cold glass.

Infrared rays are absorbed in Earth's atmosphere by water vapor and carbon dioxide, so infrared telescopes are most useful in high, dry locations.

Infrared telescopes mainly help identify the existence of relatively cool objects in the atmosphere: protostars, cosmic dust clouds, certain types of galaxies, quasars, stars in general, and comets.

How is temperature measured in space?

Astronomers can measure temperature by studying various electromagnetic radiation waves. In the United States, the Fahrenheit (F) scale is usually used to measure temperature. Most of the rest of the world uses the Celsius (C) scale. Scientists, however, use the **Kelvin (K) scale**, also known as absolute temperature.

On the Kelvin scale, 0°K = −273°C or −460°F. Water freezes at 32°F, 0°C, and 273°K. A normal live human body temperature is 98.6°F, 37°C, and 310°K. Water boils at 212°F, 100°C, and 373°K. The surface of the sun measures 10,000°F, 6,000°C, and 5,800°K. (To translate °K into °F, multiply the number of °K by 1.8 and subtract 460 from the answer. To translate °F into °C, subtract 32 from the number of °F and divide by 1.8.)

LOOKING AT CELESTIAL OBJECTS

The Triangulum Spiral galaxy, 2.9 million light-years away, is just beyond the point where it can be seen with the naked eye. With the best telescopes, astronomers are able to detect celestial objects 15 billion light-years away.

What are celestial objects?

Unless you are blinded by the bright lights of a city, the nighttime sky will show you bright lights of its own. The lights in the sky are objects emitting electromagnetic waves that we see as light. Lumped together, these objects—mostly stars, planets, satellites, comets, galaxies, and meteors—are often called celestial objects, or heavenly bodies. The word *celestial* stems from the Latin word for heavenly, caelesti. *The heavens* is a rather old-fashioned term for that corner of the universe that we can readily see from Earth.

How can you tell the difference between all the lights in the sky?

There are many ways to look at the night sky. The most obvious is to stand outside and look up. On a clear, dark night, the sky—what astronomers call the **celestial sphere**—appears filled with individual points of light. Only by studied, careful observation can you distinguish a star from a planet or one star from another.

People have been studying the night sky for thousands of years, first just by looking, then by looking through telescopes and binoculars, and now also by measuring all kinds of electromagnetic radiation besides light. By looking and studying, and with careful training, astronomers can see amazing details in what may appear to some as just another starry night.

Do the stars move?

Traditionally, people have thought of the stars as immovable and permanent, but they do move. We know the stars move because we know that the universe is expanding. But Earth is also moving in the expanding universe, so the movement of the stars is imperceptible—you can't see it.

"Wait a minute," you might say. "I can see the stars move across the sky every night. They rise in the east and set in the west, just like the Sun." Just like the Sun, however, the stars only seem to move because Earth is rotating on its axis. We are the ones who are moving.

What is the celestial sphere?

Even though we know that the heavens do not rotate around Earth—it only appears so because Earth is rotating

You can have a star named after you by purchasing the registration at most astronomy/star stores. But, beware, the registration of the star might not be recognized by the scientific community.

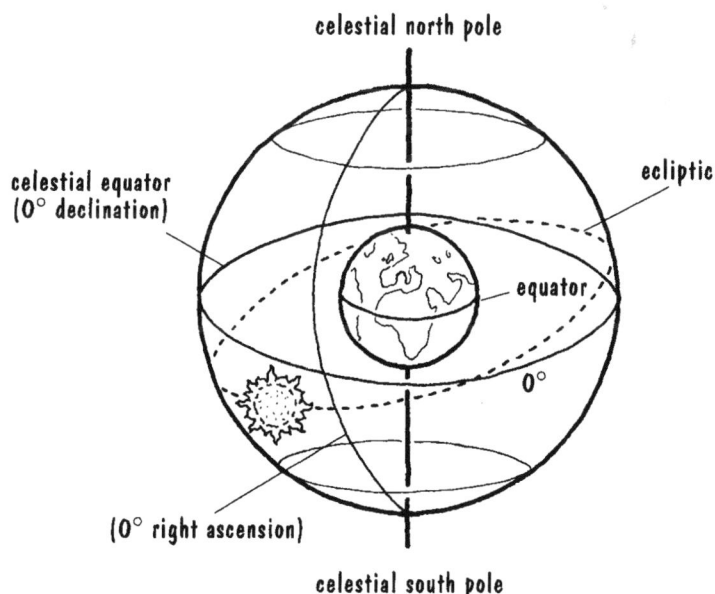

Like Earth, the celestial sphere has an equator, poles, longitudes, and latitudes. They are called the celestial equator, the celestial north and south poles, right ascension, and declination. The ecliptic is the path the Sun appears to take around Earth.

on its axis—astronomers find this image useful in locating stars, planets, galaxies, and comets. The starry sky looks like a dome high above Earth. Imagine this dome completely surrounding Earth, as if Earth were the center of a Tootsie Roll Pop. The dome is called the celestial sphere. We stand on the

inner sphere of Earth, looking up at the celestial sphere.

What is the "celestial globe?"

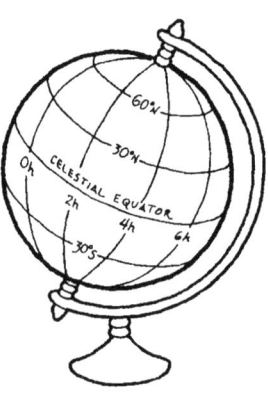

Just as we use a terrestrial globe to show geography on Earth, we can use a **celestial globe** to locate stars in space. All the visible stars are on the surface of the globe. (When you are looking at a celestial globe, you need to imagine yourself inside the globe looking out.) Since stars "move" from east to west across the sky when you spend time looking at them, the globe represents the celestial sphere at a specific point in time—as if someone took a snapshot of it—called an **epoch**.

How do you locate stars on a celestial globe?

A celestial globe is marked with imaginary vertical and horizontal lines called **declination** (dec) and **right ascension** (RA). These lines correspond to **latitude** and **longitude** lines on a terrestrial globe. Just as you can locate a town by finding the intersection of its latitude and longitude (Sonora, Texas, sits approximately at 30° north latitude and 100° west longitude), you can find a star at the intersection of its declination and right ascension: the star Arcturus is at 14 hours, 15 minutes, 40 seconds RA, 19°11′ north (or +19°11′) dec.

How is a star's declination measured?

Declination (dec) on the celestial globe is like latitude on the terrestrial globe. The celestial equator mirrors Earth's equator, halving the sphere into northern and southern hemispheres at 0°. The degrees of lines of declination increase north and south to 180° at each celestial pole (just like latitudes increase to 180° at the terrestrial North and South Poles). Fractions of declination degrees are called minutes, and are notated with a symbol called prime ('). Instead of saying north or south declination, a plus sign (+) can be used for north and a minus sign (−) for south. The star Betelgeuse can be located along the line of declination 7 degrees and 24 minutes north of the celestial equator: 7°24' north dec, or, +7°24' dec.

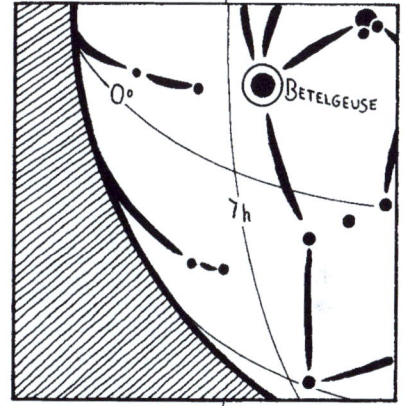

How do you measure a star's right ascension?

On the terrestrial globe we use longitude lines to express east-west location on Earth. The prime meridian and the International Date Line are the imaginary vertical lines splitting Earth into two halves. Longitudinal degrees increase from the prime meridian (0°) to the east and west until they reach the International Date Line (opposite the prime meridian), which is 180°.

The celestial globe substitutes right ascension (RA) for longitude, with the **vernal equinox** taking the place of the prime meridian. There are, however, some minor differences. RA is measured in hours (^{h}), minutes (^{m}), and seconds (^{s}); (1 hour = 15°). The hours increase all the way around the celestial globe from 0^h to 24^h, starting and ending at the vernal equinox. The right ascension of the star Betelgeuse is $05^h 55^m 10^s$ RA, or 5 hours, 55 minutes, 10 seconds around the celestial globe to the right of the vernal equinox.

What is a stargazer's zenith?

Say you are standing in your backyard. If you look straight up over your head, that is your **zenith**. It is the intersection of the imaginary north, south, east, and west lines rising from the horizon of your field of vision.

What is the celestial horizon?

When you are stargazing, the farthest you can see along the ground in any direction is called your **celestial horizon**. Just as the Sun rises over the horizon, so do all stars appear to rise and set over your celestial horizon. On a map, your celestial horizon corresponds to Earth's horizon around you, but when you are actually outside looking at the sky there are buildings, fences, trees, and many other objects that get in your line of vision.

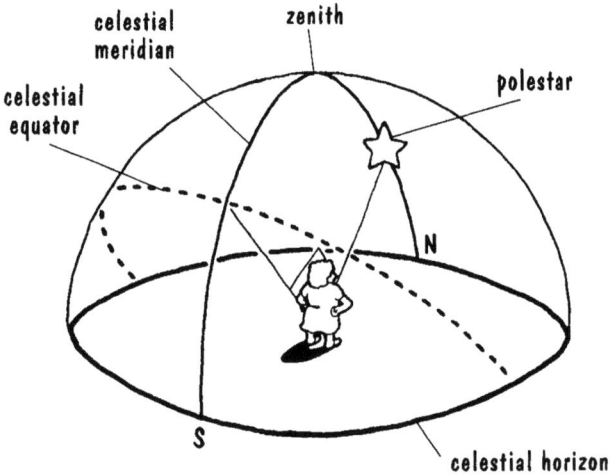

The circle around you where the sky and ground meet is called your celestial horizon. Everyone's celestial horizon is different—it depends on where you are standing.

What is your celestial meridian?

Your celestial meridian is an imaginary line that begins at the northern point of your celestial horizon and travels over your head, through your zenith, and down to the southernmost point of your celestial horizon. The line makes a hemispherical arc from north to south through your zenith. There is no special term for the east-west line through your zenith.

How can you picture the celestial globe from your specific location on Earth?

When you look up into the night sky, you see only some of the stars on the celestial globe. Some are on the other side of Earth from you, beneath your celestial horizon. To orient, or line up, your stargazing position in reference to the celestial globe, you have to imagine where your celestial horizon and zenith appear on the globe.

In the Northern Hemisphere, locate the northern celestial pole by looking into the sky above the northern point of your horizon the same number of degrees as your latitude on Earth. If you are stargazing at 40° north (Philadelphia, Pennsylvania, for example), look up along your celestial meridian 40° from the northern point of your celestial horizon. There you will find the North Star (Polaris) marking the celestial north pole. If you look 90° along your celestial meridian from the North Star—past your zenith—you will locate the celestial equator. Your zenith will be at the declination that has the same number as your latitude (40° in our example). Armed with all this information, you can find your own piece of night sky on the celestial globe. (The method in the southern half of Earth is the same, but there is no polestar that marks the south celestial pole.)

Is the North Star always the "polestar?"

Fortunately for us, the North Star (Polaris) will be the **polestar**—marking the celestial north pole—during our lifetimes. But this will not always be the case. Earth does not rotate smoothly on its axis. Imagine a spinning top. As the top slows down, it wobbles a little. Instead of its axis following a constant path, it begins to make wider and wider circles in the air, until the top loses its momentum and falls on its side. While Earth is in no danger of falling on its side, its axis does not remain in a fixed path, either. Like the axis of a slow top, Earth's axis describes a circle in the sky. The circular movement of the axis is called **precession**.

Because of precession, Earth's polar axis will point to a star other than Polaris (our current polestar) over time. But this will take thousands of years (26,000 years for one

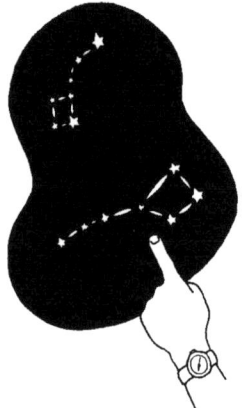

circle). In 3000 B.C., the axis pointed to Thuban as the polestar. In another 12,000 years, Vega will be the polestar.

What are constellations?

Constellations are simply groups of stars that people have named for the sake of convenience. People have been mapping constellations for thousands of years, usually naming them after mythological characters or common items that the group of stars resembles. For instance, the constellation Leo looks like a seated lion. If you were to connect the dots (stars), you would draw a rough outline of a lion.

There are eighty-eight constellations officially recognized by the International Astronomical Union. The most familiar may be the Big and Little Dippers (or the Great and Little Bear, respectively) and Orion the Hunter.

What is the zodiac?

The zodiac is a group of twelve constellations—Pisces, Aries, Taurus, Gemini, Cancer, Leo, Virgo, Libra, Scorpio, Sagittarius, Capricorn, and Aquarius—that comprise a band of the sky through which the Sun travels. The Sun's apparent path through the zodiac is called the **ecliptic**. If you imagine being able to see the Sun and stars at the same time, you would see the Sun moving through each of the zodiac's constellations over the course of the year.

When we say that we are a Gemini, or a Virgo, or a Scorpio, we are referring to the zodiacal constellation where

Leo

Hand Measurements

While stargazing, it is sometimes difficult to estimate distances in the sky. Here are a few helpful shortcuts:

(1) Raise your index finger in the air; its width is approximately 1°.

(2) Make a fist and raise it to the sky: the width is about 10°.

(3) If you spread out your fingers against the background of the sky, you have a measure of approximately 20°.

the Sun would appear on the day we were born. Zodiac signs, however, belong to the study of astrology (how the stars supposedly effect our lives), which has nothing to do with astronomy (the study of the universe).

Do stars in constellations also have names?

Yes, but just like people, stars can have official names and nicknames. For instance, the brightest star in the constellation Leo has long been called Regulus. But not every star has been given a nickname, and nowadays it seems impractical to do so. Stars in constellations are now classified from the brightest to the faintest. The brightest star is given the first letter in the Greek alphabet, alpha (α), and the possessive form of the constellation's Latin name. The next brightest star has the second letter in the Greek alphabet and the constellation's name, and so on. So, our friend Regulus is officially identified as α Leonis.

How can you measure distance by degrees looking at the sky?

Without looking at star maps as a reference, you can estimate degrees of distance in the celestial sphere by using a couple of tricks. In general, if you hold your hand in a fist vertically at arm's length, it measures about 10° against the sky. Looking from Earth, the distance between the two stars that point to the North Star—Merak and Dubhe, which form the right side of the Big

Stars within a constellation are light-years away from each other. They appear to be visually connected only when viewed from Earth.

Dipper's bowl—is approximately 5°. Also, remember that your celestial meridian—the imaginary line arcing above your head from your northern celestial horizon to your southern celestial horizon—equals 180°, and that your zenith is at 90° from the horizon.

Do stars always appear to rise in the east and set in the west?

Many of the stars you will see follow a path across the sky from horizon to horizon. **Circumpolar stars**, however, appear to circle the northern and southern celestial poles without ever rising or setting. This is because the celestial sphere appears to rotate on the axis between its poles (in fact, it is Earth that is rotating on its axis). If you draw a circle around the celestial pole in your hemisphere (the North Star in the Northern Hemisphere) at a distance equal to the number of degrees of your latitude, the stars within that circle remain above your celestial horizon all night. For example, if you are stargazing at 40° latitude, any stars within a 40° radius of the North Star do not rise or set, but are always visible traveling around the celestial pole.

What would you see if you stargazed at the North Pole?

If you were looking at stars from Earth's North Pole, the terrestrial globe would line up precisely with the celestial globe. Your celestial horizon would mirror the celestial equator. The North Star would be at your zenith, straight above your head. All the other stars in the northern hemisphere of the celestial sphere would appear to travel in circles around the sky, neither setting nor rising.

Do stars rise and set when seen from Earth's equator?

If you are stargazing at the equator, your celestial horizon is at right angles to the celestial equator. The North Star hovers on your northern celestial horizon. All the stars seem to rise and set at right angles to your celestial horizon, and there are no circumpolar stars.

Do stars rise and set at the same times every night?

You may notice that when you are stargazing in your yard at 10:00 every night, the stars appear slightly to the west of where they were the night before. Stars rise 4 minutes earlier every night, and set 4 minutes earlier. Therefore, over the months, the starry night changes. Over the period of a year, those minutes add up to 24 hours, so that every 12 months, the same stars show up at the same positions in the sky.

The difference in the stars' rising and setting times results from Earth's rotation around the Sun. The celestial sphere remains relatively still, but Earth moves around the Sun. The stars appear to be in a different place at the same time each night because, in fact, you are in a different place in space every night. Because it takes 365 days for Earth to rotate around the Sun, you have 365 slightly different night skies to study.

How can we measure the distance of a star from Earth?

In the same way that survey-ors measure distances of unchart-ed land—by creating three points of a triangle—astronomers mea-sure the distances of the stars. Mathematically (using trigonome-try), if you know the length of the baseline of a triangle and the arc of two of its angles, you can

What Time Is It?

There are two kinds of time in astronomy: **solar time** and **sidereal time.** Ordinary clocks (and this book) use solar time, based on Earth's rotation and orbit in rela-tion to the Sun. The foundation of sidereal time is Earth's rotation only, in relation to stars other than the Sun. Neither method of keeping track of time is more accurate than the other. They are simply two differ-ent methods of organization.

A solar day is 24 hours long, but Earth actually takes only 23 hours, 56 minutes, and 4 seconds to make one complete rotation on its axis. Because of the orbital distance Earth travels over the course of one axial rotation, it takes an extra 3 minutes and 56 seconds for the Sun to appear in the same place (at high noon) in the sky every day. The length of a sidereal day disregards this orbital distance and equals exactly one Earth rotation: 23 hours, 56 minutes, and 4 seconds.

According to solar time, the stars appear in the sky approximate-ly 4 minutes earlier with every pass-ing night. Using sidereal time, the same stars appear in the same place at the same time every night.

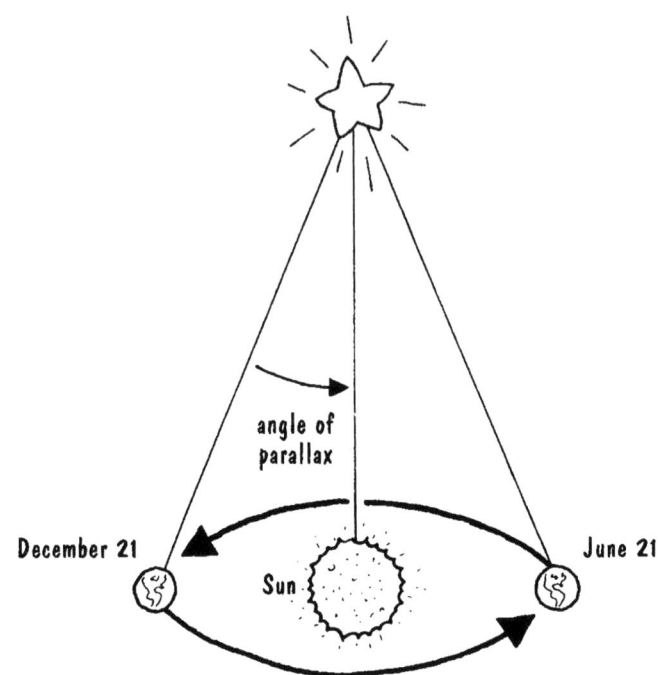

December 21

angle of
parallax

Sun

June 21

To measure the distance to a star, astronomers create an imaginary triangle between Earth, the star, and Earth again, when it has completed
one-half of its orbit. Knowing the two base angles, they calculate the
third (parallax) angle. From the angle measurements, they compute
the distance to the star.

figure out the distance to the third point of the triangle,
and thus the arc of the third angle.

Because stars are so far away, the triangles needed to
compute their distance must be vast. Astronomers use the
average diameter of Earth's orbit around the Sun—93 million miles × 2, or 186 million miles—as the baseline of
their celestial triangle. They pinpoint a star in the sky one
night, and then again exactly 6 months later (when Earth
is on the opposite side of its annual orbit around the Sun).
This gives them the information needed to figure out the
star's distance and parallax, or degree of angle between
the two sides of the triangle stemming from the baseline.
(Once the parallax is determined, astronomers cut it in
half. This equals the parallax angle using the radius, not the
diameter, of Earth's orbit as the baseline of their triangle.)

THE UNIVERSE AND ITS GALAXIES

What is the universe?

The universe is a dynamic, evolving organism. It had a beginning—probably a sudden, massive expansion of matter—and it may have an end. We don't know. Meanwhile, it grows by means of further expansion; galaxies move farther and farther away from each other. The universe is filled with activity and motion. Stars explode into existence and expand and contract throughout their lives. Planets revolve around stars. Galaxies spin and tumble. Comets and asteroids streak through solar systems. Elements, atoms, molecules, and particles constantly interact, creating change. Electromagnetic waves are everywhere. Yet, for all we can see out there, it may be that most of the universe is made of dark matter, which we have not been able to find.

What is cosmology?

Cosmology is the study of the evolution and structure of the universe. It includes big questions: How did the universe begin? Will the universe end? How will the universe end? How do the components of the universe interact? Does the universe have boundaries? Today's theories about the universe are built upon careful observation, study, and debate; mathematics and physics; and original thought.

How did the universe begin?

The most popular theory about the universe's creation is called the **big bang theory**. It is based on the ideas of many scientists, especially Edwin Hubble, a famous twentieth-century astronomer. The big bang theory claims that the universe was created by a massive surge of energy and matter 10 to 20 billion years ago. The big bang formed celestial gases and particles—and everything that exists.

The theory also states that the universe continues to expand, that all the celestial bodies—galaxies, stars, and planets, to name a few—are constantly moving away from each other.

What types of particles did the big bang create?

In the immediate aftermath of the initial rapid "vavoom" that started it all (scientists say the big bang was not an explosion, but a burst or surge) very little matter existed. Immediately after, subatomic particles combined to create protons and neutrons. Protons and neutrons form the nucleus of atoms. The first atoms were of hydrogen and helium. From the basic interactions of these two elements, all other matter—including you—was formed.

How does the universe expand?

Unfortunately, we can't get outside the universe to see what it looks like as it expands, but we can imagine it. If you took a balloon and marked it with dots and then blew up the balloon, the dots would expand along with the balloon's surface. As the balloon grew larger, the dots would move away from each other, just as the galaxies do in our universe.

Will the universe continue to expand forever?

Current theories say this depends on how much physical matter exists in the universe—and we aren't sure just how much stuff there is. The amount that would keep the universe stable is called **omega**. Omega is a hypothetical, unknown quantity of matter, but scientists have determined what is likely to happen if there is more or less

How to Blow Up the Universe

Try this exercise to visualize the universe as astronomers see it. Take a deflated balloon and draw small stars on it with a marker. The stars represent galaxies. Label one the Milky Way, for our galaxy. Now, blow up the balloon. The growing balloon is similar to the expanding universe. You will see how the stars spread out, which is something like the way galaxies move apart. The air inside the balloon represents the past; the balloon surface represents the present; and the air surrounding the balloon represents the future.

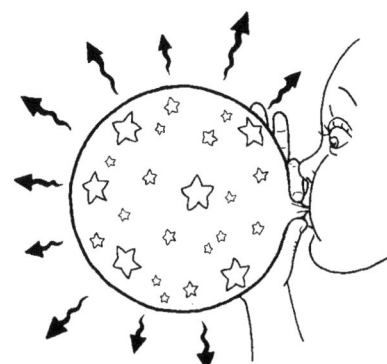

Blowing up a balloon dotted with "galaxies" can give you an idea of how the universe is expanding.

matter than the omega amount. If there is less matter than omega, the universe will continue to expand and the matter will continue to cool as it grows farther and farther apart. Stars will eventually die out, leaving all matter dark and cold, and always moving away from other matter. This concept of a constantly expanding universe is known as the **open universe model**.

If there is more matter than the omega amount, the forces of gravity (every bit of matter exerts gravity on other matter) will sooner or later slow and stop the expansion. Gravity will cause the matter to draw together and the universe will begin to contract. At some point, the universe will then fall in upon itself. This is called the **closed universe model**, nicknamed the **big crunch**.

Will the big crunch be the end of the universe?

We don't know for sure what the end will be like—or whether there will even be an end. The big crunch theory refers to gravity causing everything in the universe to contract and collapse in upon itself. There are two results that scientists generally propose. Either matter will collapse into a mammoth **black hole**, and that will be the end of the universe, or the big crunch will lead to another big bang and the creation of another universe (or maybe the same universe all over again!).

What is a black hole?

This fascinating hypothetical concept does not refer to a hole in the proper sense of the word. A black hole is an object, a massive amount of energy in a tiny amount of space. Very large stars, much more massive than the Sun, for instance, will likely end their existence by collapsing to a size of just a few miles in diameter. The concentrated gravitational force of a black hole pulls in all matter within its reach. All matter includes all atoms, subatomic particles, and electromagnetic waves—even light.

What is the cosmological constant?

Some scientists theorize that the amount of matter is not the most important factor in the fate of the universe. They explain that a cosmological constant will keep the universe forever balanced between infinite expansion and inevitable collapse.

One view of the cosmological constant, known as the **steady state theory**, holds that new matter is created at roughly the same rate as old matter dies out. In another, the **flat universe model**, the rate of expansion and the force of gravity will even each other out—regardless of the amount of mass—so that the universe will come to a point of rest and stay there.

How much matter is in the universe?

Since the force of gravity relates precisely to the mass of an object, we can estimate the mass of the universe by observing the forces of gravity in the universe. We also can add up the known mass of different atoms and particles in the universe. The problem is that when astronomers add up the mass of all the objects they can see and all the objects they can't see but know exist, they still come up short. We can only account for about 6 or 7 percent of the mass we know is needed for the universe to behave the way it does. The mass we haven't yet found is called **dark matter**.

What is dark matter?

The bulk (at least 90 percent) of matter in the universe, making up its mass, is a mystery. We don't know what it is, and not all scientists believe that dark matter exists.

All matter we know about is made up of particles called **photons** and **neutrons**. Photons and neutrons are the building blocks of what we call **baryonic matter**, or ordinary matter. It is likely that a portion of dark matter is made of something we have never identified, or **non-baryonic matter**. There may be building blocks of matter that are so different from what we know that we can't even find them.

How big is the universe?

As far as scientists can tell, the universe measures between 10 and 20 billion light-years in diameter. The size of the universe, however, changes every instant—that is, if we believe one of the most widely accepted twentieth-century theories postulating that the universe is expanding.

What is a galaxy?

A galaxy is a loose formation of stars (between 1 million and 1 trillion), dust, and gases. These stars, dust, and gases are drawn together in clusters by their forces of gravity, much in the same way as our solar system is held together by the gravity of the Sun and the planets.

How many galaxies are there?

Galaxies are the largest, most prominent structures in the universe; however, our telescopes may not be powerful enough to count all of them. With data from the Hubble Space Telescope, a telescope high above Earth's atmosphere, scientists recently revised their estimate of the number of galaxies from mere billions to at

You can't possibly see all the stars in our galaxy. Billions of them are hidden by dust and gas, and others are too distant to be seen clearly; their lights blend together to give the galaxy its hazy impression.

The word galaxy *comes from the Greek word* gala, *meaning "milky," because galaxies look milky, or cloudy, when clustered together.*

least hundreds of billions. With better telescopes, we may find even more.

How do astronomers study galaxies and figure out what happened billions of years ago?

By studying galactic light that originates 300 million light-years away, astronomers can look at galaxies that are 300 million years younger than the Milky Way. (The light we see today started traveling 300 million years ago, so it represents the source galaxy as it was 300 million years ago.) Galaxies at different distances portray different stages of galactic evolution.

Are there different kinds of galaxies?

Although all galaxies are composed of the same things, each one is unique. Some galaxies are mostly made up of clouds of dust and gases. Others contain more stars than clouds. Galaxies can appear flat or spherical.

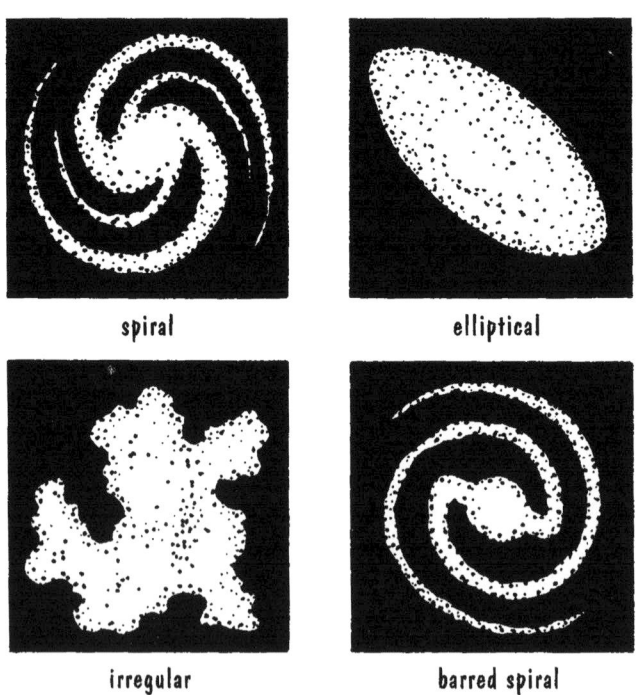

spiral   elliptical

irregular   barred spiral

Astronomer Edwin Hubble classified galaxies according to shape: elliptical, irregular, or spiral (spiral is further divided into normal or barred spirals). The Milky Way is a spiral galaxy.

Some are bright and clear; others are dim and obscure. Galaxies can stand alone or interact with other galaxies in clusters. Perhaps most important of all, galaxies are not fixed. They not only travel as the universe expands, but they rotate on their axes and orbit other galaxies, as well. Neighboring galaxies sometimes join each other; larger galaxies cannibalize, or consume, smaller ones. Stars within galaxies are constantly changing as they are born, reach maturity, and die out.

In spite of all their differences, however, most galaxies share common characteristics and can be categorized by shape as one of three types: spiral, elliptical, or irregular.

How are spiral galaxies described?

Spiral galaxies, such as our own Milky Way, look something like pinwheels. They have a central, circular, cloudy-looking mass of stars with arms spiraling out from the center. Barred spiral galaxies have bar-shaped centers with arms coming off from the ends of the bars. The spiral shape seems to be left over from the motion of the big bang. Old, middle-aged, and young stars are all found in spiral galaxies, along with a lot of gas and dust.

What are elliptical galaxies like?

Elliptical galaxies have the shapes of ellipses, or stretched-out circles. They can be egg-shaped, almost round, or almost flat. The astronomer Edwin Hubble created a scale from 0 to 7 to designate the roundness of an elliptical galaxy. An elliptical galaxy that is almost round is called E0, while one that is almost flat is E7. Elliptical galaxies contain mostly old stars, with little gas and dust.

What are irregular galaxies?

Galaxies that do not share a common shape fall into the catchall category of

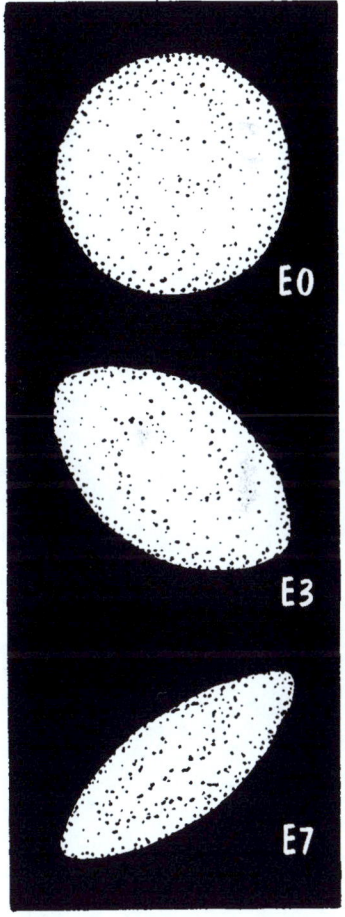

Elliptical galaxies come in gradations of roundness. Edwin Hubble's classification of galaxies designates the different varieties E0 to E7, counting from most round to almost flat.

irregular galaxies. They are populated mostly by young stars, though old ones also appear, as well as gas and dust.

What does our galaxy look like?

We live in the Milky Way Galaxy. Sometimes, on dark, clear nights, you can see part of the Milky Way as a cloudy, or milky, river of stars in the night sky. Our solar system happens to be on the edge of the galaxy—the Sun is about 30,000 light-years from the center—so we are able to see a pretty good side view.

If we were able to view our galaxy from far away, it would look like a huge swirl of stars, with a center shaped like the yolks of two floating fried eggs stuck back-to-back. This center is called the nuclear bulge. We can't see or photograph the whole galaxy from the outside, but pictures of other galaxies similar to ours help us to understand the Milky Way. The Andromeda Galaxy, some 2.2 million light-years away, is thought to be almost a twin of the Milky Way.

The Milky Way looks something like two fried eggs stuck back-to-back. The yolks would be the nuclear bulge and galactic halo (the spherical region around the galaxy); the whites would be the spiraling arms.

What is the Milky Way's center made of?

The nuclear bulge of the Milky Way cannot be seen clearly from Earth. Using the Andromeda Galaxy as a visual guide to our own, we believe that the nuclear bulge is a collection of star clusters and clouds of dust and gas. The detection of gamma ray, X ray, infrared, and radio waves gives us more information. Something in the nuclear bulge emits powerful radio waves; huge streams of very hot gas shoot out from the center. Some astronomers believe that a black hole exists at the Milky Way's center. We don't, however, have the instruments or knowledge yet to say exactly what is in the middle of this swirling galaxy.

What details do we know about the Milky Way?

The Milky Way is a spiral galaxy that is estimated to be between 10 and 20 billion years old. It is about 100,000 light-years at its widest and 15,000 light-years at its thickest in the center. It contains more than 100 billion stars (maybe even 200 billion), most of which are concentrated in the nucleus and spiral arms. Most stars are grouped with stars of similar ages.

What is interstellar medium?

Interstellar medium is the term for the gas and dust that exists between stars. Gas makes up 99 percent of interstellar medium; dust, only 1 percent. Radio waves have shown that most of the gas is made of hydrogen (75 percent) and helium (23 percent), with smaller amounts (2 percent) of carbon monoxide,

Our Nearest Galactic Neighbors

Even with the naked eye, we can see beyond our galaxy to others in the Local Group, a cluster of about thirty galaxies of which the Milky Way is one. Our twin galaxy Andromeda is visible even though it is more than 2 million light-years away. The Large and Small Magellanic Cloud barred galaxies are one-third and one-sixth the size of our galaxy, respectively, but are the brightest galaxies visible without telescopic equipment. The larger cloud (169,000 light-years away) is connected to the smaller (190,000 light-years away) by a stream of gas and dust some 300,000 light-years long. The Triangulum Spiral, nicknamed the Pinwheel, which lies at the outer edge of the Local Group, some 2.9 million light-years away, can't quite be seen with the naked eye, but can be viewed through binoculars.

carbon, oxygen, sodium, iron, nitrogen, and titanium. All
of these elements are commonly found on Earth. The dust
is more difficult to break down, but seems to contain
graphite (carbon) particles and icy crystals of water,
ammonia, and methane (all are also found on Earth).

What are nebulae?

Nebulae is the Latin word for *clouds* (**nebula** is the
singular form). They are simply very dense areas of gas
and dust (interstellar medium). Nebulae are 1,000 times
more dense than regular masses of interstellar medium.

Why do nebulae have different colors?

There are three kinds of nebulae, based on the light
they reflect. Emission nebulae glow greenish-yellow and
red. This is caused by the nearby presence of one or more
extremely hot stars. The ultraviolet radiation from the stars
causes the hydrogen and oxygen of the nebulae to glow.
Reflection nebulae contain one or more cooler stars.
Instead of the nebulae gases glowing, they reflect the
bluish light emitted by the stars. Emission and reflection
nebulae can exist in the same nebula. Dark nebulae have
no nearby stars to light the gases. They appear as dark
patches in the sky.

Is the Milky Way Galaxy moving?

The Milky Way must be rotating in order to create its
spiral shape (otherwise gravity would make all the particles merge into more of a spherical shape). While the
galaxy itself rotates on its axis—sort of rushing head over
heels through space—all the stars within the galaxy rotate
around its center. Our solar system takes one **galactic
year**—about 225 million years—to make one revolution
around the center of the galaxy.

What are star clusters?

Although some stars travel alone in galaxies, most are
grouped in star clusters. **Open** or **galactic clusters** contain between 10 and 10,000 stars loosely distributed over
15 to 40 light-years. Most of the stars are relatively young,
bright, and hot. Open clusters appear within the galactic

*Planetary nebu-
lae were first
thought to be
clouds of mat-
ter destined to
become plan-
ets—hence the
name. They are,
in fact, stars
that are in their
last stages of
dying out.*

*Astronomers
estimate that
there are be-
tween 100 and
200 billion
stars spread
throughout
our galaxy.*

plane—the nucleus and spiral arms. **Globular clusters** have between 100,000 and 1 million stars, densely packed within the space of 75 to 400 light-years. There are only about 150 globular clusters in the Milky Way and they inhabit a spherical region around the galaxy called the galactic halo. Stars in the globular clusters are some of the oldest stars discovered in the galaxy.

When were the galaxies formed?

Astronomers believe that all of the galaxies were formed around the same time, 10 to 20 billion years ago. They probably came into existence only a few hundred million to a billion years after the big bang.

How did the galaxies form?

There are many theories about galaxy formation; most of them contain the basic notion that there must have been gravitational seeds, regions that had more mass (and, hence, more gravity) than everything around them. Those seeds evolved into the galaxies of today.

Early discussions of the big bang theory included the idea that all matter initially expanded in a uniform, smooth manner because nothing existed to interrupt its journey. Scientists have since theorized that before sub-atomic particles combined to form hydrogen and helium, the first two elements, particles may have clumped togeth-er—that there were in fact variations in the distribution of matter. These clumps of the most basic particles would have had more mass and hence more gravity than non-clumping particles. They would have attracted more and more matter, eventually creating stars. The stars' gravity would attract other stars, forming galaxies.

Another interesting theory postulates that at the beginning of the big bang, there existed energy fluctuations called cosmic strings. These fluctuations would be similar in nature to the energy transition of water to ice. Water and ice have the same atomic structure, but repre-sent different forms of energy. The cosmic strings would disrupt the otherwise uniform energy of the big bang. Just as the clumps mentioned above could act as seeds for galaxies, so could the cosmic strings.

What are quasars?

Quasars are the farthest identifiable objects from Earth. Because, in space, distance equals age, they are also the youngest objects. Discovered in 1960, quasars seem to be very small (about the size of our solar system) and very luminous (some are brighter than 100 galaxies put together). Quasars can travel at an incredible speed—over 160,000 miles per second.

Many astronomers believe that for quasars to be so small, and yet so bright and powerful, they are probably very early, very active galaxies powered by black holes at their centers. A black hole can have the mass and energy of a billion suns in the diameter of only 5 light-hours, so the presence of a black hole at a quasar's center would explain its speed and power.

Quasars' young age and great activity have led some scientists to think that they are somehow related to the birth of galaxies, but we do not have enough information to know if this is true.

How are galaxies spread out through the universe?

Most galaxies are grouped together in clusters. These clusters contain anywhere from just a few to thousands of galaxies. Within clusters, galaxies orbit each other at speeds of about 600 miles per second. In turn, galactic clusters often come in groups called **superclusters**, which can be as large as 1 billion light-years in length.

The Milky Way Galaxy is one of more than thirty galaxies located in the cluster known as the **Local Group**, extending about 3 million light-years across. The Local Group is in the **Local Supercluster** along with about fifty other clusters centered around the Virgo cluster some 60 million light-years away.

Virgo

What exists between galactic superclusters?

The regions between superclusters—called **voids**—generally contain no galaxies. Voids make up approximately 95 percent of the universe. Contrary to what you may think, voids are probably far from empty. Some astronomers believe that most of the matter in the universe resides in the voids, probably in the form of dark matter.

Do galaxies interact?

For a long time, scientists thought that galaxies were quiet, stable citizens of the universe. On the contrary, however, many galaxies engage in great, even violent, activity. **Seyfert galaxies**, for instance, emit 100 times the electromagnetic waves of ordinary galaxies. **Active galaxies** are known to collide and produce massive nuclear explosions, sending jet streams of matter stemming from their centers.

When two galaxies get too close to each other in their orbits, the larger galaxy, or **cannibal galaxy**, will frequently consume the smaller. Evidence of this cannibalism is seen in the form of a large galaxy exhibiting more than one nucleus. The nuclei are left over from the devoured galaxy. A galaxy named Abell 407, for instance, has nine nuclei from galaxies it has swallowed.

The nucleus of a galaxy is a powerful source of energy. It is commonly thought that some galaxies, including the Milky Way, may each have a black hole at their centers.

STARS AND THE SUN

What are stars made of?

Stars are made mostly of hydrogen and helium, along with small amounts of calcium, iron, and titanium oxide. The amounts of these elements differ from star to star. Astronomers can tell what elements are in a star, and how much of each, by studying the various wavelengths of a star's electromagnetic radiation.

How bright are stars?

There are three ways to talk about a star's brightness. We can discuss the **apparent magnitude** of a star, or how bright it appears when we look at it. We know, however, that stars nearer the earth *appear* brighter than far-away stars, even though they may not actually *be* brighter. So, astronomers also talk about the **absolute magnitude** of stars, or the brightness of a star if the observer were 10 parsecs from it. The third way to measure a star's brightness is called **luminosity**. Luminosity is a measure of how much energy a star puts out in comparison to our Sun.

How is a star's apparent magnitude measured?

Apparent magnitude, or how bright a star appears when we look at it, is always defined in comparison to another star.

An increase in apparent magnitude by a factor of 1 means that a star is 2.5 times brighter than another star.

Comparison of apparent magnitude of Rigel and Pollux

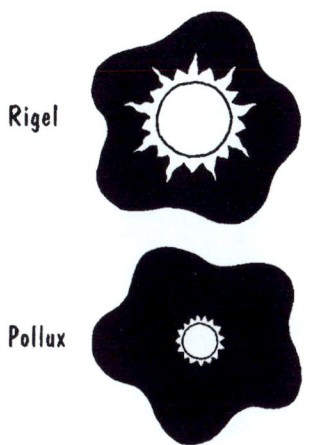

Rigel

Pollux

Rigel, in the constellation Orion, lies some 900 light-years away from Earth. In Gemini, the star Pollux is about 40 light-years away. The fact that Pollux outshines Rigel is not surprising, given the difference in their distances. If Pollux and Rigel were both at the same distance from Earth, however, Rigel would be about twice as bright as Pollux (as shown).

The star Rigel appears brighter than the star Pollux; Rigel has an apparent magnitude of 0.12 and Pollux's apparent magnitude is 1.14. Rigel appears approximately 2.5 times brighter than Pollux (1.14 − 0.12 = 1.02).

Stars that have negative magnitude numbers are brighter than stars with positive magnitude numbers. For instance, the following stars are in order from brightest to faintest in terms of apparent magnitude: the Sun, (−27.72), Alpha Centauri (−0.27), and Altair (0.77). Usually, the closest star appears to be the brightest star and the furthest appears to be the faintest: for example, the Sun is 93 million miles away, Alpha Centauri is 4.3 light-years away, and Altair is 16 light-years away. Sometimes a very bright star that is far away will outshine a closer star: Canopus, 80 light-years away, has an apparent magnitude of −0.72, far brighter than nearby Alpha Centauri.

What is a star's absolute magnitude?

When we look at stars, the closer ones usually appear brighter than the ones farther away. Absolute magnitude is how bright each star would look if they were all 10 parsecs

Star Bright, Brighter, Brightest

Stars seem fainter or brighter depending on their size and distance from Earth. See for yourself how these factors make a difference by trying this experiment.

Equipment
  flashlight
  one piece of paper
  one piece of aluminum foil

1. Cut a hole the size of a small coin in the aluminum foil. Keep the foil with the hole in it for future use.
2. Put the paper on the floor of a dark room.
3. Shine the flashlight over the paper from a distance of about 2 feet (62 cm). Note the light's brightness on the paper.
4. Shine the flashlight over the same paper at a distance of 12 inches (31 cm). Note the increased brightness.
5. Cover the flashlight with the foil so that the light will shine through the hole. Shine the light on the paper from the height of 12 inches (31 cm). The light is even brighter still.

You have tested the effects of distance and size on the brightness of light. Now you probably can understand more clearly why astronomers use two different measures to record a star's brightness: apparent and absolute magnitudes. Apparent magnitude is how bright a star looks from Earth. Absolute magnitude is how bright stars would be if they were all at the same distance (10 parsecs) from Earth.

(33 light-years) away. For instance, the Sun appears to be the brightest star. It has an apparent magnitude of −27.72. Altair appears about sixty-five times fainter than the Sun, with an apparent magnitude of 0.77. But if both stars were 10 parsecs away, the Sun's magnitude would be 4.8 and Altair's would be 2.3. The Sun's absolute, or true, magnitude is 7.5 times fainter than Altair's. (Remember that higher magnitude numbers mean fainter stars.)

What is luminosity?

Luminosity (L) is the measure of energy (power) emitted by a star. It is measured the same way we measure the energy output of a lightbulb. Lightbulbs come in different strengths: 40 watts, 60 watts, or 100 watts, for instance. (A watt is a unit of energy emission.) The Sun's luminosity, or energy output, is about the same as 4,000 billion trillion 100-watt light-bulbs. One degree of luminosity (1 L) is equal to the Sun's luminosity. The star Sirius has a luminosity of 30 (30 L). It puts out thirty times more energy than the Sun.

How are stars classified?

Different stars have different surface temperatures, depending on their chemical composition, size, and age. Astronomers have developed seven basic classifications for stars according to temperature, which are called **spectral classes**. From hottest to coolest, the classes are O, B, A, F, G, K, and M. Class O stars have surface temperatures greater than 30,000°K (53,540°F/29,727°C). Class M stars have temperatures less than 3,500°K (5,840°F/3,227°C).

The Brightest Stars

The following table compares the apparent and absolute magnitudes of important stars.

Star	Apparent magnitude*	Absolute magnitude**	Distance
Sun	−27.72	4.8 (10)	93 mil. miles
Sirius	−1.46	1.4 (8)	8.6 lt-yr
Canopus	−0.72	−2.5 (2)	80.0 lt-yr
Alpha Centauri	−0.27	4.1 (9)	4.3 lt-yr
Arcturus	−0.04	0.2 (7)	34.0 lt-yr
Vega	0.03	0.6 (5)	25.0 lt-yr
Capella	0.08	0.4 (6)	41.0 lt-yr
Achernar	0.46	−1.3 (3)	69.0 lt-yr
Hadar	0.61	−4.4 (1)	320.0 lt-yr
Pollux	1.14	0.7 (4)	40.0 lt-yr

* In order by apparent magnitude from the brightest to the faintest.
** Numbers in ( ) indicate order by absolute magnitude from the brightest to the faintest.

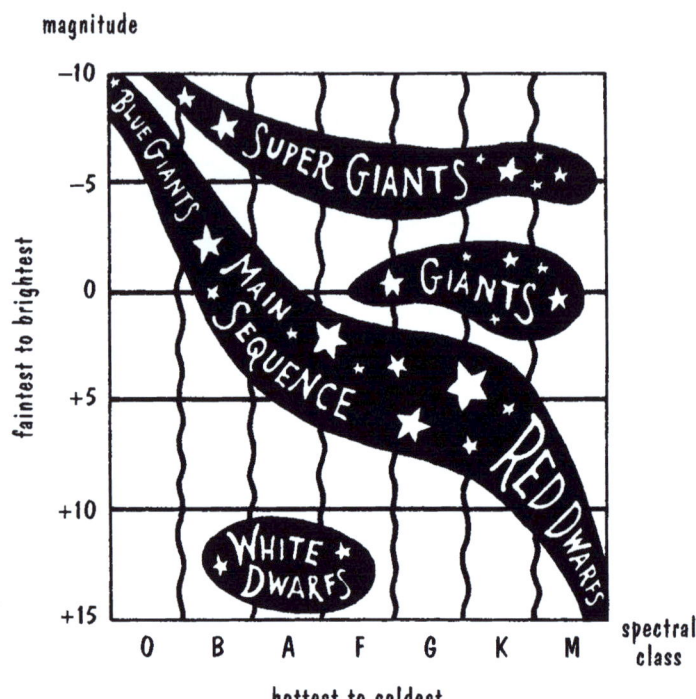

magnitude

faintest to brightest

spectral class

hottest to coldest

The Hertzsprung-Russell diagram shows the correlation between temperature of a star (O to M) and its magnitude (–10 to +15). Mature stars, such as the Sun, are found along the main sequence. Old stars—giants and super giants—are bright, but cool. They generally end up as hotter, but darker, white dwarfs.

(The other classes fall in between.) The Sun is a class G star, the class of stars whose temperatures range from 5,000° to 6,000°K (8,540° to 10,340°F/4,727° to 5,727°C).

What is the Hertzsprung–Russell diagram of stars?

Two scientists—Ejnar Hertzsprung and Henry N. Russell—discovered the connection between a star's luminosity, absolute magnitude, and temperature. They created a graph, called the **Hertzsprung-Russell diagram**, on which all stars can be plotted according to these three characteristics. When stars are put onto the graph, 90 percent of them fall along one diagonal path, showing that there is a definite relationship between how hot a star is

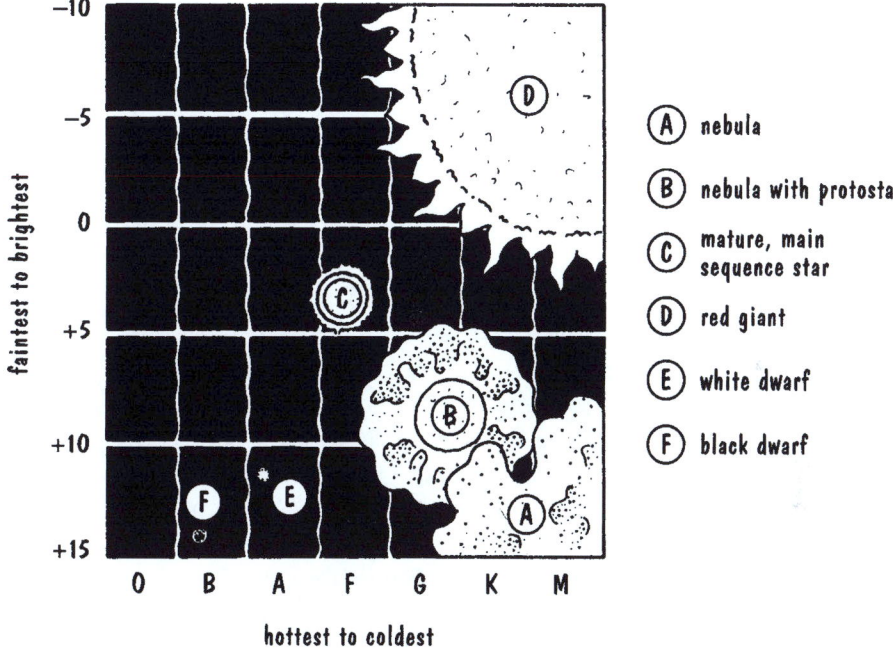

		A	nebula
		B	nebula with protostar
		C	mature, main sequence star
		D	red giant
		E	white dwarf
		F	black dwarf

hottest to coldest

At the beginning and end of its life, a typical star will be dark (for example, +15), but as a mature and dying star, it may reach great magnitude (for example, –10). Likewise, a star will move back and forth through many spectral classes, M class being the coldest and O class the hottest. A star's mass largely determines its magnitude and temperature.

and how bright and luminous it is.

Astronomers refer to stars along this path as **main sequence stars**. Cooler, less bright/luminous main sequence stars are called **red dwarfs**. Hot, very bright/luminous main sequence stars are referred to as blue giants. Stars not on the main sequence that are both cool and very bright/luminous are super giants or **red giants**. A few other stars, not on the main sequence, are hot, but not bright/luminous. They are called **white dwarfs**.

What are the stages of a star's life?

Stars can be said to go through the same stages of life as people: birth, infancy, maturity, old age, and death. As with people, stars are not all the same. The differences in their lives—their spectral class, life expectancy, and eventual end—depend primarily on their mass, or the amount of matter they have.

How is a star born?

Space is full of clouds of dust and gases, known as nebulae. The dust and gases in nebulae have a certain mass, and we know, from Newton's law of gravity, that any object with mass attracts other objects to it. The dust and gases are gradually pulled toward each other by the force of gravity. In this early stage of creation, a star is called a **protostar**.

The protostar doesn't look anything like what we think of as a star. It is too cold and loosely packed to give off any light. Technically, it has been born, but its matter must first collapse under its own gravity and begin thermonuclear fusion before we would recognize it as a fully realized star. Astronomers know about protostars because they radiate radio and infrared waves.

What is a new star?

A new star, or protostar, does not yet shine. It is a loose mass of cold dust and gases. Gravity forces the protostar to contract during its infancy, which lasts for millions of years. A protostar trillions of miles (kilometers) wide will shrink to only millions of miles (kilometers) in diameter. The motion of the shrinking protostar creates an enormous amount of pressure and heat. When the temperature of a protostar reaches 10 million°K (about 18 million°F/10 million°C), it stops contracting. The process of **thermonuclear fusion** begins, which produces the star's energy. The protostar has become a star and begins to shine.

What is thermonuclear fusion?

Stars are mostly made up of hydrogen atoms. At 10 million°K (about 18 million°F/10 million°C), the nuclei of hydrogen atoms fuse (join together) and change into helium. It takes four hydrogen atoms to change into one atom of helium. Some of the star's mass is lost as it converts into energy, but the energy continuously created through thermonuclear fusion is what feeds the star throughout its maturity.

What is a mature star?

A star's maturity is marked by its presence on the main sequence of the Hertzsprung-Russell diagram. Where it first appears on the main sequence, however, depends on its mass. A star with greater mass will be hotter, take less time to mature, and will appear on the upper part of the diagram. A star with less mass will be cooler, take longer to show up, and will appear lower down on the main sequence.

It took the Sun about 30 million years to age from a protostar to a main sequence star. The average temperature of the Sun is approximately 6,000°K (10,000°F/ 6,000°C). A star three times the size of the Sun will mature in about 1 million years, and will be more than twice as hot. A star about one-tenth the mass of the Sun will take about 100 million years to appear on the main sequence and will be half as hot as the Sun.

How long does a mature star live?

This depends on how much mass the star has. Stars feed themselves by turning hydrogen into helium. Through this process, they lose mass. You could say a star consumes itself to stay alive. It spends 90 percent of its life doing so.

Hot, bright blue giants have more hydrogen turning into helium all at once. They die fastest, spending only a few million years as a mature star. Cool, dim red dwarfs have less hydrogen. They consume their mass more slowly and can live for billions of years. The Sun, which is of average size, temperature, and brightness, has shone for about 5 billion years already. It has another 5 billion years or so to go as a main sequence, or mature, star.

When do stars leave the main sequence?

When stars have used up most of the hydrogen in their cores (through thermonuclear fusion), they leave the main sequence and pass into old age. Most stars, the Sun included, will turn into red giants or super giants.

What happens when a star becomes an old star?

The core of a red giant or super giant (an old star) is mostly helium, with an outer shell of burning hydrogen. The helium contracts while the hydrogen expands. The star grows brighter and much bigger as the hydrogen escapes into space as radiation. Expansion cools the shell, but contraction heats the core. When the core reaches 100 million°K (180 million°F/100 million°C), the helium turns into carbon through another process of thermonuclear fusion. Within a few hours, the core's increasing heat and energy set off a helium flash. The helium flash—not quite an explosion—sparks yet another string of nuclear reactions, and, for the next few million years, the star moves back and forth—toward and away from—the main sequence.

What are variable stars?

Three types of variable stars grow brighter and dimmer at regular intervals: Cepheids, RR Lyrae, and long-period variables (LPVs). These stars are probably between old age and death.

Cepheids take anywhere from about 1 to 70 days to go from their brightest to their dimmest and back to their brightest. The brightness of RR Lyrae varies during regular cycles that average less than 1 day. LPVs' brightness fluctuates at irregular intervals longer than 80 days. The cycle for the LPV named Mira, for example, takes more than 300 days.

How does a star's life end?

The end of a star's life depends on its mass. Small stars die pretty quietly, becoming **planetary nebulae**, white dwarfs, and then black dwarfs. Very large stars explode in **supernovae**, possibly turning into **neutron stars** or black holes.

What are planetary nebulae?

After a red giant has used up its helium, its outer layer is thrown off into space. The jettisoned shell, made up mostly of hydrogen, is called stellar wind. The star's deeper layers form an expanding shell, about 0.5 to 1 light-year wide, known as a planetary nebula. Early astronomers wrongly thought that these masses were **protoplanets**, hence the adjective "planetary." The planetary nebula expands and dissipates quickly, leaving the core behind as a white dwarf.

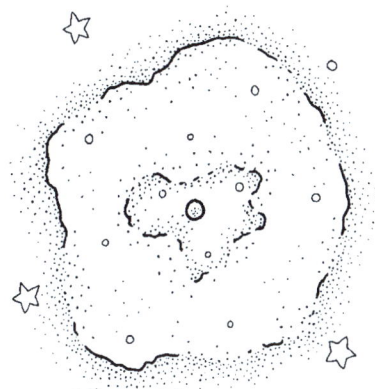

What is a white dwarf?

The core of an old star that has lost most of its outer mass is called a white dwarf. It is mostly carbon, with a relatively thin shell of burning helium. The core temperature remains too low to produce nuclear fusion, so the atoms simply continue to contract. The atoms then break down under the compression of gravity until they are little more than nuclei. (A white dwarf once the size of the Sun can squeeze into a space the size of Earth. Even a teaspoonful of the densely compacted matter of a white dwarf would weigh several tons on Earth.) Its dim light comes from its burning outer shell.

If you were to put a teaspoonful of the core of a white dwarf on your head—as if to shampoo your hair—it would flatten you like a steamroller.

How do white dwarfs become black dwarfs?

Eventually, the helium shells of most white dwarfs burn themselves up and their core temperatures and luminosities drop. Finally, the stars simply die out, leaving behind cold balls of carbon called **black dwarfs**.

What is a nova?

Many stars travel in couples called binary star systems. When one of the stars becomes a white dwarf, its force of gravity sometimes attracts matter from its companion star. This causes the white dwarf to flare up briefly but brilliantly as a **nova**, but there is no lasting effect.

What is a supernova?

A star many times more massive than the Sun ends life in a spectacular explosion called a supernova. Whereas the core of a smaller star turns into carbon too cool to create nuclear fusion, the core of a massive star becomes hot enough to spark carbon fusion. Carbon fusion turns the core into a steel-like ball. At 600 million°K (1 billion°F/600 million°C), a carbon flash ignites the star's explosion.

What is left after a star explodes?

Scientists hypothesize that the leftover core of a supernova would be like the entire Sun squeezed into an area 10 miles (16 km) wide. The remaining core, called a neutron star, would be made of neutrons, atoms stripped of their electrons (electrical charges), and would lack the energy to emit light. The particles of carbon, oxygen, and nitrogen shot off into space during the explosion —at about 5,000 miles (8,000 km) per second—may become part of new stars or planets.

What are pulsars?

Scientists have not recorded any stars that have actually become neutron stars, but they have found pulsars. **Pulsars** are invisible sources of strong, regular bursts of radiation (mostly radio waves). According to astronomers, these pulses come from places where neutron stars *should* exist, based on the evidence of celestial matter, electromagnetic radiation, and gravitational forces in the area. These pulsars have the highest density of any celestial object located so far, which is compatible with the idea of the mass of a huge star squeezed into a small space. They act and appear as theoretical neutron stars would—as rapidly spinning invisible loci of great electromagnetic waves. Many scientists believe that pulsars are, in fact, neutron stars.

How could stars become black holes?

Black holes were first discussed in 1783, but their existence has not been proven beyond a shadow of a doubt. Astronomers theorize that if a large mass were squashed into a tiny space, the resulting power of gravity would attract and devour all nearby matter, even light. It would be a black hole. Black holes are not actually holes in space. They are objects.

The first likely black hole—Cygnus X-1, in the constellation Cygnus—was found in 1965. Since then, many other powerful objects too massive to be neutron stars and too small to be regular stars have been designated as black holes.

Theoretically, the gravity of a very massive star (with at least three times more matter than the Sun at the time of its collapse) would cause the star to continue to contract beyond the stage of being a neutron star. That star would have a terrific gravitational pull; it would be a black hole. For instance, if the Sun shrank to a sphere with a 2-mile (3-km) radius, it would become a black hole. (While not a star, the Earth would have to collapse to a radius of 0.4 inches [1 cm] to become a black hole.) No nearby matter could then escape the pull of its gravity—not even radiation.

Why haven't black holes been found?

Astronomers have not been able to verify the presence of black holes precisely because no radiation—nothing—can escape their gravitational force. Evidence of their existence relies on activity in the environment around a suspected black hole: all matter and radiation being sucked toward a specific point and disappearing.

Invisible Objects

Astronomers don't always have evidence of a celestial object itself, but must rely on their knowledge of the neighborhood of a suspected object, such as a black hole or neutron star. For instance, they may see a patch of sky where everything—all light, all radiation—appears to be streaming to one point. Perhaps the point of convergence is a black hole. Or, maybe astronomers find the remains of stellar wind—the ejected residue of a nova (the explosion of an old star). They can't see where the stellar wind came from, but they detect regular bursts of electromagnetic waves from an apparently superdense object. Maybe they have found a neutron star.

Research like this may seem haphazard compared to scientific laboratory experiments, but the universe is not a controlled environment. Astronomers must rely on a vast array of data to come up with their findings—and they do with amazing precision.

What kind of star is the Sun?

The star nearest to us, the Sun, is a mature star. It is classified as a red dwarf. In terms of spectral class, it is a G star. Its absolute magnitude is +4.8, so it is of average brightness for a star. Because the Sun is so close to Earth, it looks like the brightest star in the universe; so its apparent magnitude is −27.72.

How old is the Sun?

We don't know the exact age of the Sun. It probably took some 30 million years for it to form out of gas and dust and make its way onto the main sequence. The Sun has been shining for about 5 billion years and has enough mass to fuel itself for another 5 billion years before it begins to decline.

Are Astronomers Wrong About Stars?

Probably not, but one piece of evidence is lacking from astronomers' theory of thermonuclear fusion within stars. Thermonuclear fusion, which creates solar energy, releases a great quantity of subatomic particles called **neutrinos**. Huge numbers of them ought to come from the Sun. After careful experimentation, however, astronomers have found only 10 percent of the neutrinos they expected. The fact that neutrinos are missing from the Sun leaves a big question mark. As a result, astronomers have to consider that they may be wrong about what happens inside the core of a star.

How will the Sun die?

Scientists expect that after another 5 billion years, the Sun will have used up its hydrogen energy supply and will begin to burn helium. At that point, the Sun will likely grow to become a red giant, big enough to encompass the orbit of Mars. Like other red giants of its size, its outer layer will disperse as stellar wind, leaving its core to cool and dim as a white dwarf. Eventually, when its core is cold and dark, the Sun will be a black dwarf.

What is the Sun made of?

Like other stars, the Sun is composed mostly of gases. About 70 percent of the gas is hydrogen and 25 percent is helium. Just like other stars, the Sun's hydrogen produces energy by changing into helium through the process of thermonuclear fusion.

We see the Sun's energy in the form of sunlight and feel it as heat.

How big is the Sun?

The Sun measures 865,000 miles (1,392,000 km) in diameter. It would take more than 1.3 million planets the size of Earth to fill the Sun. On a scale, the Sun would weigh almost 333,000 times more than Earth; its mass is 2×10^{27} tons.

Earth has different layers; does the Sun have them, too?

At the center of the Sun lies its core, where hydrogen fuses into helium, creating energy. The core is estimated to be about 280,000 miles (450,000 km) in diameter. From the core out, there is the radiative layer, more than 167,000 miles (278,000 km) deep; the convection layer, about 125,000 miles (200,000 km)

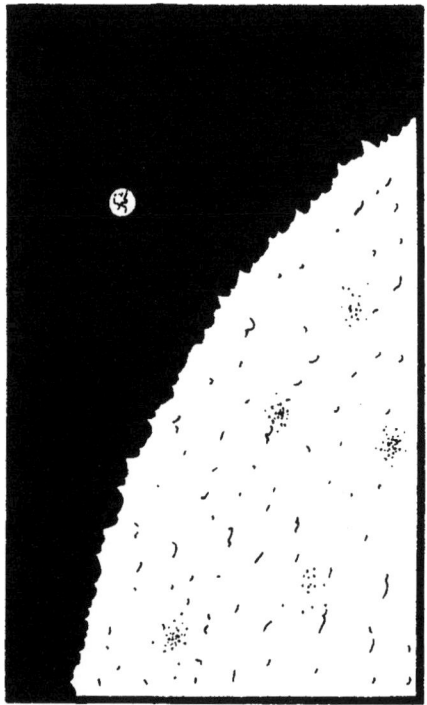

The Sun is 1.3 million times larger than Earth, but is considered just average-sized compared to other stars.

deep; and the **photosphere**, about 190 miles (300–500 km) deep, which we see as the Sun's surface. The Sun's atmosphere is made of the chromosphere, nearest the surface, and the outer corona.

Why does the Sun shine?

The Sun, a main sequence star, is at a stage of its life during which it is fueled by thermonuclear fusion. In this process, hydrogen converts to helium, creating massive amounts of energy. Just as with all the stars we see shining in the sky, some of this energy radiates as visible light—rays of sunlight.

How hot is the Sun?

The core temperature may register as high as 15 million°K (27 million°F/15 million°C), which is 1.5 times

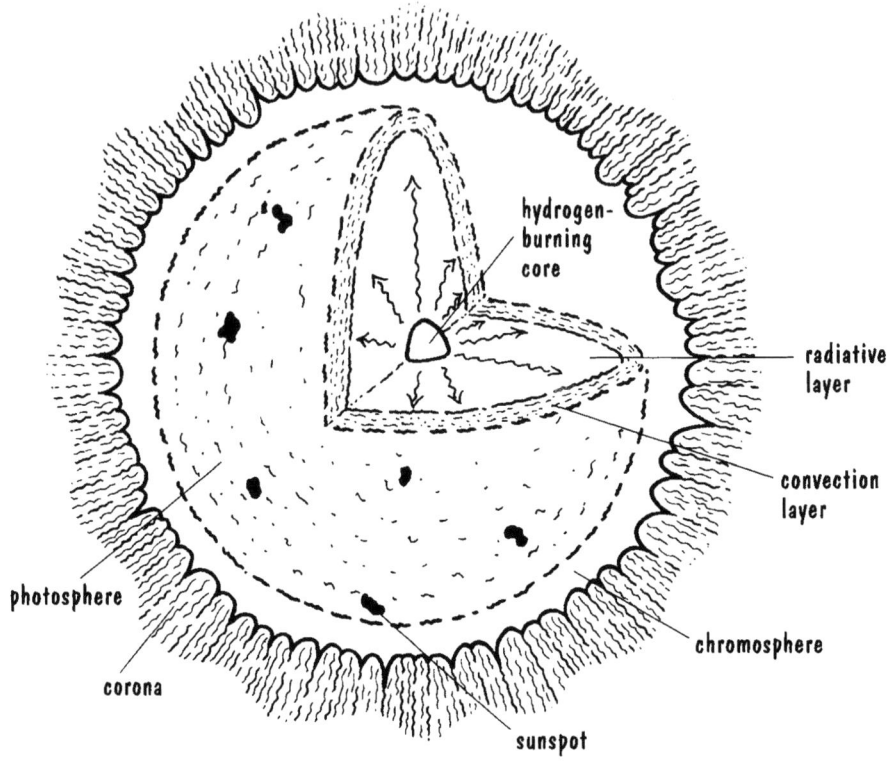

hydrogen-
burning
core

radiative
layer

convection
layer

photosphere

chromosphere

corona

sunspot

The Sun's layers are not solid, or molten, like Earth's, but are comprised of swirling, active gases and particles of matter. Hydrogen and helium, which fuel the Sun's thermonuclear reactions, are the star's main components.

"hotter" than a nuclear bomb explosion. While the surface is much cooler—only 5,800°K (10,000°F/6,000°C)—it's still some twenty times hotter than the temperature at which paper burns.

How can we look at the Sun?

It is necessary to discuss looking directly at the Sun because every year people damage their eyes by not taking precautions—especially during eclipses. This is no joke. Looking at the Sun, even for a few seconds, with the naked eye or through binoculars or telescopes may result in blindness—permanent or temporary—or other damage to your eyes.

Two accepted ways to view the Sun are by projecting the Sun's image through a telescope onto a screen, and

Never look at the Sun through binoculars, telescopes, or with the naked eye. The light and heat is so strong that you could be blinded!

then studying the screen, or by using a manufactured filter over the objective lens—not the eye-piece—of a telescope.

Does the Sun move?

We see the Sun rise and set each day, but sunrise and sunset occur because Earth is moving—rotating on its axis—not the Sun. The Sun, however, does move. As the universe expands, all galaxies—and the Sun is part of the Milky Way Galaxy—are mov-ing away from each other. The Sun (and the whole solar system) also revolves around the center of our galaxy once every 225 mil-lion years. In addition, the Sun rotates on its axis. The gas around its equator makes one rotation about every 25 days while the gas around its poles rotates once about every six days.

What is a solar eclipse?

A **solar eclipse** occurs when the Moon (at its new Moon phase) passes between Earth and

Don't Look Directly at the Sun!

It's so tempting to look at the Sun during an eclipse, especially when everyone tells you not to. Doing so, however, can damage your eyes. Here's an alternative way to view an eclipse, without injuring your eyes.

Equipment
   a covered cardboard box
   a pin
   scissors

1. Punch a hole in the top of the box with the pin. Cut an eyehole in one end of the box.
2. Go outside. Raise the box to your eye and move it around until the Sun is shining directly through the pinhole. You should be able to see the image of the Sun on the bottom of the box.
3. During the eclipse, watch the Sun's image as the Moon crosses in front of the star. You will see the eclipse as it takes place.

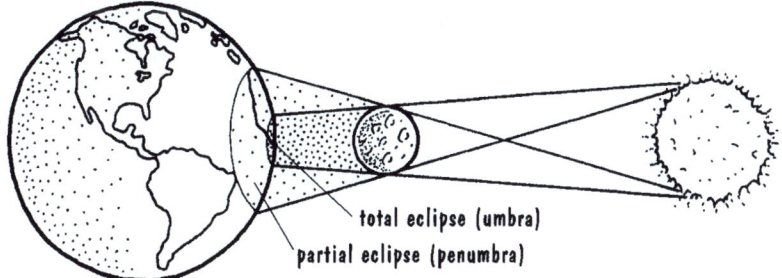

total eclipse (umbra)
partial eclipse (penumbra)

The syzygy (alignment) of the Earth, full or new Moon, and Sun causes the Moon to block our view of the Sun in an eclipse. The area of Earth experiencing a total eclipse is said to be in the umbra, or shadow, of the eclipse. The areas at more of an angle to the eclipse are said to be within its penumbra, or outer shadow.

Solar Eclipse

total eclipse   **partial eclipse**   **annular eclipse**

A total eclipse leaves only the Sun's corona visible. A partial eclipse creates the illusion that the Sun is a crescent. An annular eclipse differs from a total eclipse only in that the Moon is at its farthest point of orbit from Earth. At that distance (maximum: 252,000 miles [406,000 km]) the Moon is too far away from Earth to completely cover the Sun's surface, and we can view the Sun's annula.

the Sun. When viewed along the eclipse path, the Moon completely blocks out the surface of the Sun when it is close to Earth (the alignment of the Sun, the Moon, and Earth is called **syzygy**). This is called a **total solar eclipse**. A partial solar eclipse is seen when the Moon is not quite in direct alignment between the Sun and Earth. An annular eclipse happens when the Moon crosses between the Sun and Earth when it is at a greater distance from Earth; its sphere is then not large enough to completely hide the Sun's surface. During an annular eclipse, the Sun's annula, or outer ring of its surface, is visible.

What can we see on the surface of the Sun?

The center of the Sun appears brighter than its edges because it is hotter. The Sun's heat is evidence of the star's energy. The constant energy, fueled by thermonuclear fusion, can be seen on its surface in undulating waves, called **granules**. But the energy is not always stable; it fluctuates in intensity. Some disturbances of energy create **sunspots**, the cooler, darker patches seen on the Sun's photosphere. The Sun displays bursts of enormous energy in hot, bright faculae, flares, prominences, and spicules.

Is the surface of the Sun smooth?

The vast distance to the Sun makes its surface look smooth from Earth, but, on the contrary, the Sun's photosphere is bumpy. The Sun is made of turbulent hot gases, rising from the interior. The movement of the gases creates an undulating surface, which looks something like the skin of an orange. Every bump of the orange skin would represent a moving gas current, known as a granule. The currents each last about 8 minutes and spread out approximately 600 miles (1,000 km) in diameter. About 4 million currents exist on the Sun's surface at any given time.

What causes a sunspot?

Sunspots seem to be visual evidence of magnetic disturbances in the Sun's convective or radiative layers. In other words, sunspots are areas of highly intense magnetic energy, which are dark because they are much cooler than their surrounding areas. They usually occur in pairs, and sometimes in groups. The center of a sunspot, known as the umbra, is very dark; the edges, or penumbra, are lighter.

The first historical evidence of a sunspot sighting comes from the fourth century B.C. At first, people believed that sunspots were planets orbiting the Sun, until Galileo declared that the spots were actually on the Sun's surface.

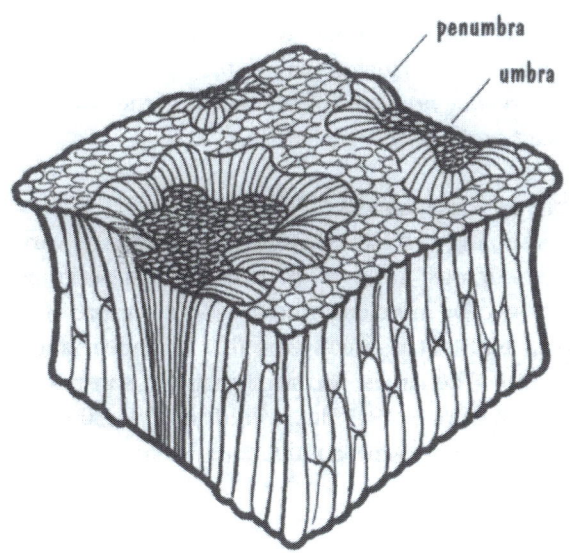

penumbra

umbra

The umbra is the center, or darker area, of a sunspot. The brighter penumbra forms a "shadow" around the umbra.

Are sunspots permanent?

Sometimes you see them and sometimes you don't. Individual sunspots come and go within days or weeks, the newer ones appearing closer to the equator. Sunspot activity, however, has an average cycle of 11 years. (Some scientists claim that 11 years is only one-half of a full 22-year cycle.) The cycle begins with the appearance of sunspots between 35° and 40° of latitude from the solar equator. The height of the cycle occurs about 4 years later when a great number of sunspots appear around the 15° latitude lines. By the time sunspots begin to show up within about 5° of the equator, about 7 years later, the cycle is at an end (and a beginning, as new sunspots reappear between 35° and 40° of latitude). Sunspots appear to travel horizontally across the surface of the Sun, but this is simply evidence of the Sun's rotation.

Some scientists propose that sunspot activity may effect weather on Earth. During the Maunder Minimum, London's Thames River froze over most winters—quite a rare occurrence in England's temperate climate.

How regular are sunspot cycles?

The cycles take an average of 11 years, though intervals as short as 7 years and as long as 17 years have been recorded. Not every cycle displays the same number or size of sunspots. In particular, between A.D. 1645 and 1715—an era dubbed the Maunder Minimum after British astronomer E. W. Maunder, who detected it—sunspot activity was scarce. Fluctuations in the cycle are likely to occur again, but no one knows whether they will have any impact on Earth.

How big are sunspots?

These strange shadows on the Sun's surface vary in size and groupings. About 75 percent of sunspots come in groups of two or more, with one leading umbra, or center dark patch, that is usually the first to appear and the last to vanish. The largest recorded group of sunspots was measured on April 8, 1947. It covered some 11,300 square miles (18,000 square km), a little more territory than in the state of Maryland.

What are faculae?

These hot areas that appear on the Sun's surface are actually clouds of hydrogen just above the photosphere.

Faculae can be easily seen when at the edge, or **limb**, of the Sun's disk, but are difficult to distinguish toward the center of the star. The word *faculae* comes from Latin and means "torches." As with sunspots, we don't know much about faculae.

Are sunspots and faculae related?

There may be some connection between these two solar phenomena. While sunspots are cooler, darker patches of the photosphere, faculae are hotter, brighter areas. Faculae always appear a few hours or days before new sunspots develop. Sunspots at the edge, or limb, of the Sun's disk, are accompanied by faculae. Faculae, however, also appear without sunspots, frequently at the Sun's magnetic poles.

What causes solar flares?

Sunspots have great magnetic forces, which fluctuate in intensity and polarity as does Earth's magnetic field. When the magnetic field of a sunspot loses its stability, it can cause a violent explosion, called a flare. Flares look like sudden brilliant stars within a star, generally lasting less than an hour. The explosion sends shock waves through the chromosphere (the layer above the surface), releasing energy, massive radiation, and particles of the

prominence

flare   spicule

Flares, prominences, and spicules are abrupt outbursts of the incredible energy within the Sun. The Sun's energy is fueled by thermonuclear fusion—like the destructive energy of a hydrogen bomb. These solar displays can be seen only with special equipment designed for astronomers to protect their eyes.

Sun. If it weren't for the protection of Earth's atmosphere, the incoming radiation—especially the dangerous ultraviolet and X rays—would cause the complete extinction of life on the planet. As it is, such solar activity creates massive atmospheric magnetic storms and can damage spacecraft and supersonic jets.

What do prominences look like?

Prominences appear as flaming arches at the limb, or edge, of the Sun's disk. Electrically charged gases in prominences come from the magnetic fields around sunspots. Prominences last for weeks or even months, and arc tens of thousands of miles (km) into the Sun's chromosphere.

What are spicules?

Tall, vertical streams of gas, called spicules, are like huge fiery geysers shooting up into the Sun's chromosphere and then disappearing. They rise about 6,000 miles (10,000 km) and last between 5 and 15 minutes.

The main difference between solar flares and solar wind is that the flares are localized, abrupt, and massive emissions of radiation and particles, whereas solar wind is constant and relatively less intense.

Is solar wind like wind on Earth?

Solar wind refers to streaming electrically charged atomic particles that constantly escape from the Sun through coronal holes, which are weak spots in the Sun's magnetic field. It is faster and much hotter than Earth's wind. Solar wind is traveling at about 1 million miles (1.6 million km) an hour by the time it gets close to Earth. If it blew on the Earth's surface, it would obliterate all life, but Earth's magnetic field and atmosphere protect the planet.

What are auroras?

Particles jettisoned from the Sun during a solar flare or contained in the solar wind can reach Earth in a matter of hours or days. Above Earth's North and South Poles, the planet's magnetic field is strongest and the atmosphere is filled with particularly highly charged atoms. The interaction of solar and atmospheric particles results in brilliant displays of light called **auroras**. Auroras look like bands or sheets of bright light. They can be seen almost anywhere, but appear most clearly in the night sky above the Arctic (aurora borealis, or northern lights) and Antarctic (aurora australis, or southern lights).

What does the Sun's corona look like?

The Sun's corona, or outer layer of atmosphere, can only be seen during a solar eclipse. At other times, the brightness of the Sun makes the corona disappear from sight—just as the Sun's light makes it impossible to see stars in the daytime. Astronomers artificially block the Sun's surface with special equipment (so as not to damage their eyes) in order to study the corona.

The corona can extend more than 1 million miles (1.609 million km) around the Sun. Its shape changes with the appearance of sunspots. When the sunspots are at the height of their cycle, the corona is almost circular. At the end of the sunspot cycle, the corona appears stretched out, with huge streams of gases coming out. The corona is always thinnest at the Sun's northern and southern magnetic poles.

Auroras appear at their most spectacular above the Arctic Circle in the Northern Hemisphere and below the Antarctic Circle in the Southern Hemisphere because Earth's atmosphere is most highly charged above the magnetic north and south poles.

What is the solar system?

Generally, the solar system could be said to contain everything that revolves around the Sun, which lies at its center (hence its name—*solar* means "sun"). The solar system is made up of comets, meteors, and dust; the minor planets, or asteroids; the nine known planets—Mercury, Venus, Earth, Mars, Jupiter, Saturn, Uranus, Neptune, and Pluto—with their satellites; and, of course, the Sun.

How big is the solar system?

There is no definite boundary to the solar system. The center of the system is the Sun. The farthest identifiable bit of the solar system may be an icy cloud formation called the Oort Cloud from which comets appear. It extends about 2 light-years away. The nearest star to the Sun is Alpha Centauri, 4 light-years away, which may have its own solar system. By combining this information and splitting the distance between the two stars, we come up with a probable answer: the solar system is about 2 light-years in radius.

How old is the solar system?

The solar system did not form all at once. We know that the Sun started shining about 5 billion years ago, but the planets came afterwards. Astronomers estimate that Earth was likely formed some 4.6 billion years ago and that the other planets, asteroids, and satellites coalesced at about the same time. It is safe to say that the solar system as a whole is about 4.6 billion years old.

What is a comet made of?

A comet is often described as a dirty snowball. A comet's **nucleus** (solid core) is, in fact, made of 50 percent dust and gases, and 50 percent ice. The dust is made up of rock and metal; the ice is actually frozen gas. Both are believed to be left over from when the solar system formed some 4.6 billion years ago.

What are the parts of a comet?

Our knowledge of comets is based on what we see as they travel nearest the Sun in their orbits around the star. Except for comets with relatively short orbits, we don't know how far or precisely where else they travel. As a comet nears the Sun, the ice in the nucleus begins to melt,

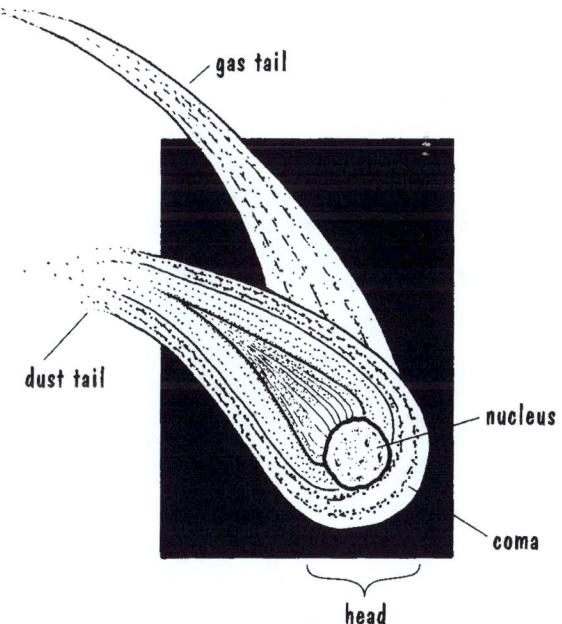

As a comet nears the Sun in its orbit, its rock-and-ice nucleus decomposes (sometimes completely). Solar wind blows dust and gases away from the comet's head in two tails. There are two tails because the densities of dust and gases react differently to the force of the solar wind.

*The head
of the comet
Flaugergues,
discovered in
1811, is big-
ger than the
Sun.*

creating a huge gaseous cloud called the coma. The
nucleus and the coma together are called the head. At the
same time, the solar wind blows particles of comet dust
and gas into separate tails. The tail of gas can extend hundreds of millions of miles (km), while the dust tail is generally shorter. (While comets have two tails, they are
commonly perceived as one by nonastronomers, and are
often referred to in the singular "tail," rather than "tails.")

Why does a comet's tail sometimes precede the comet?

The gas and dust in a comet's tail are extremely light-
weight. The tails are created by solar wind rushing past the
orbiting comet and blowing material away from the defrost-
ing coma. When the comet approaches the Sun, the force
of the wind pushes the tail out behind the comet. When the
comet is moving away from the Sun, the wind still rushes
past it, now sending the comet's tail out in front.

Where do comets come from?

Comets probably come from the **Oort Cloud** and
the **Kuiper Belt**. These aren't places in a science fiction
book! The Oort Cloud, named after astronomer Jan Oort,

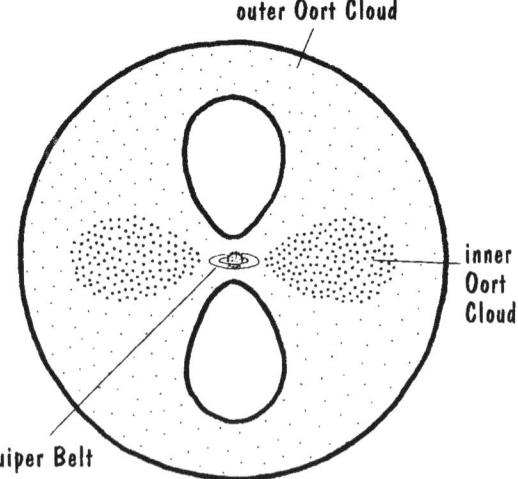

Most comets are believed to come from the Oort Cloud, an outlying
area of the solar system. Short-period comets may originate in the
Kuiper Belt, a theoretical "junkyard" of celestial debris just beyond the
orbit of Neptune.

What's in a Name?

Some comets may come from the Kuiper Belt, but most probably originate in the Oort Cloud. The celestial bodies in the Kuiper Belt, however, prompt debate over the differences between planets, planetesimals, and asteroids.

Astronomer Gerard Kuiper studied the satellites of the outlying planets and, in the 1940s, discovered the moons Miranda and Nereid of Uranus and Neptune, respectively. He proposed the existence of a group of celestial bodies beyond the orbit of Neptune, later named the Kuiper Belt. Are these bodies asteroids, planetesimals, or planets? It is sometimes hard to say, since their composition, sizes, and orbits are loosely similar. Some astronomers question whether the planet Pluto and Uranus's moon Triton aren't in fact just large planetesimals (leftover material from the planets' formation). A number of asteroids from the Kuiper Belt, such as Pholus and 1992 QB, discovered in 1992, have eccentric orbits, and may be considered planetesimals. The fine lines between the definitions of these celestial bodies leave ample room for discussion.

is theoretically a loose shell of leftover matter from the solar system's formation. Approximately 98,000 astronomical units (AUs) thick, it encircles the Sun beginning about 2,000 AUs away.

The Kuiper Belt, theorized by astronomer Gerard Kuiper, is purported to be a band of planetesimals from the solar nebula that lies just beyond Neptune's orbit. Some comets may originate there.

Why do comets orbit the Sun?

Comets are probably ejected from the Oort Cloud or Kuiper Belt as a result of a collision. Once disturbed, they are caught by the Sun's gravity and fly into an orbit around the star. Comets that orbit the Sun once every 200 years, or less, are called short-period comets, and probably come from the Kuiper Belt or the Oort Cloud. Comets that take longer than 200 years are called long-period comets, and probably come from the Oort Cloud. Some comets do not have a periodic orbit at all, but swing around the Sun only to go flying off into space forever.

Are comets' orbits consistent?

Comets' orbits are not reliable. While the paths of more than 100 short-period comets have been mapped, astronomers can suddenly "lose" a comet. Sometimes it is simply gone. Other times, when it is found, it isn't always as expected. The Wilson-Harrington comet, discovered in 1949, was expected to return in 1952. It wasn't seen again until 1979, and then it came back resembling an asteroid instead of a comet.

Selected Periodic Comets

Name	Period (years)
Encke	3.3
Halley	76.1
Kopff	6.5
Temple	5.3
Wolf	8.4

Are comets likely to collide with Earth?

Cometary orbits are not steady and orderly like planetary orbits. Comets can come from any part of the sky on any trajectory. The chances of a planet getting in the way are pretty good, especially since a planet's gravity will draw a nearby comet toward it. On June 30, 1908, a comet was reported to have crashed in Russia's Siberian wilderness. (Recent reports have raised a question as to whether it was a comet or an asteroid.) Its nucleus vaporized in the atmosphere, but the tremors from its impact were detected.

What happens if Earth goes through a comet's tail?

Earth is more likely to pass through the tail of a comet than to collide with a comet head on. After all, a tail can be millions of times larger than the nucleus. Passing through a tail doesn't have any great effect—beyond a good meteor shower—since comets' tails are severely lacking in density. In 1910, however, when Earth went

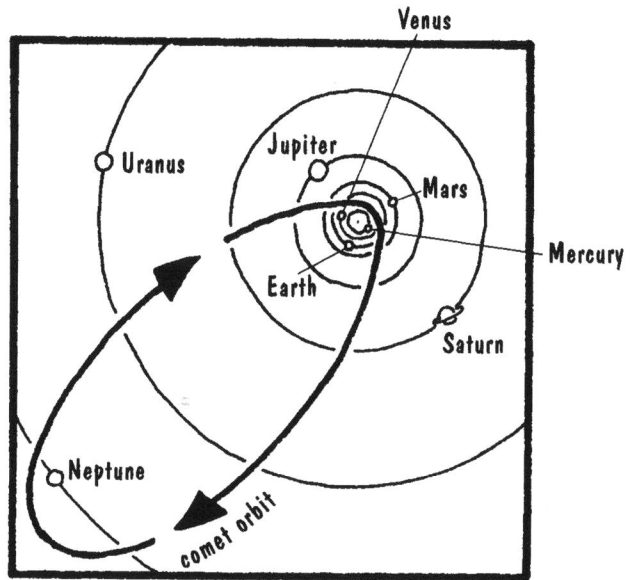

Halley's comet, probably the most popularly famous comet, completes a single orbit around the Sun about every 76 years. It will next be at its closest point to the Sun in the year 2061.

through the tail of Halley's comet, people spent good money on remedies for the expected consequent illnesses and disaster.

Do comets last forever?

Whenever a comet makes a pass around the Sun, it loses some of its matter. The ices melt and the dust streams off in a tail. Inevitably, the comet will be reduced to a meteor or to celestial confetti, or resemble an asteroid (a burned-out comet). Some comets collide with the Sun or a planet. Others break up under the pressure of gravity into two or more comets. Still others have a parabolic or hyperbolic—no-return—orbit that shoots them out of the solar system, and we don't know what happens to them.

Are comets related to meteors?

Meteors are pieces of celestial debris of any size. They can be found just about anywhere in the solar sys-

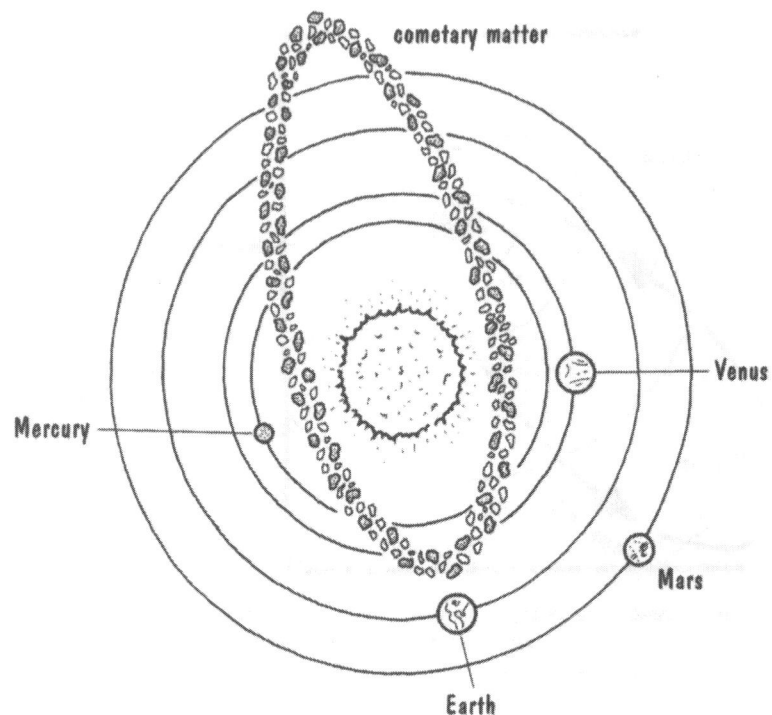

cometary matter

Venus

Mercury

Mars

Earth

A comet in orbit near the Sun leaves a great deal of broken-up matter in its wake after it is gone. When Earth, following its own orbital path, crosses the path of the comet's orbit, it passes through all the leftover debris. The cometary matter forms splendid displays of shooting stars, more properly called meteor showers.

tem. Comets are a great source of meteors because they leave particles along their paths. When Earth orbits through the cometary residue, Earthlings can see the dust fall in **meteor showers**, also known as shooting or falling stars.

What do meteor showers look like?

Meteors in a meteor shower seem to radiate from a single point in the sky—like water gushing from a showerhead as you look straight up at it. The particles of debris streak across the sky as they fall from that central point, called the radiant. Meteors actually travel parallel to each other. They give the illusion of coming outward from a central point in the sky the same way that railroad tracks appear to come from a single spot on the horizon.

How many meteors can be seen in one night?

Not all meteors come in showers. Under clear, dark skies, you should be able to see five or six meteors a night—if you stay up all night. During an annual shower—or a storm—you can see hundreds a night.

When can you see meteor showers or storms?

Earth passes annually through cometary orbits, which are littered with leftover particles. The consequent meteor showers are plentiful and heavy. The showers known as the Perseids display up to sixty-eight meteors an hour at its peak around August 12; the Eta Aquarids, around

Meteor showers occur as Earth travels through the orbital path of a specific comet; for example, the Orionids are associated with the orbital path of Halley's comet, the Perseids with the comet Swift-Tuttle's path.

Major Annual Meteor Showers

Name	Date (approx.)	number of meteors/hr max.	avg.
Quadrantids	January 3–4	110	30
Corona Australids	March 16	N.A.	N.A.
Lyrids	April 21–23	12	8
Eta Aquarids	May 2–6	20	10
Ophiuchids	June 20	N.A.	N.A.
Capricornids	July 25	N.A.	N.A.
Delta Aquarids	July 27–30	35	15
Piscis Australids	July 30	N.A.	N.A.
Alpha Capricornids	August 1	N.A.	N.A.
Iota Aquarids	August 6	N.A.	N.A.
Perseids	August 11–12	68	40
Draconids	October 9	N.A.	N.A.
Orionids	October 20–21	30	15
Taurids	November 4–8	12	8
Andromedids	November 14	N.A.	N.A.
Leonids	November 16–17	10	6
Phoenicids	December 4	N.A.	N.A.
Geminids	December 13–14	58	50
Ursids	December 22	N.A.	12

May 5, average about ten an hour, up to a maximum of twenty, and is associated with Halley's comet. The Leonids, peaking around November 17, vary from year to year, but are usually weak. In 1866, 1933, and 1966, however, they stormed. In 1966, meteors rained at a peak rate of 60,000 to 100,000 per hour, though the shower lasted only 40 minutes. Another Leonid storm is expected in 1999.

How do meteor showers get their names?

They are given the name of the constellation in which the radiant appears. The Perseids, for example, are seen in the constellation Perseus; the Geminids in Gemini; and the Orionids in Orion.

Are meteor showers dangerous?

Most meteors burn up long before they reach Earth's surface. Shooting stars, as they are nicknamed, first appear about 70 miles (115 km) above Earth. They die out by the time they are 40 miles (65 km) above Earth.

Meteorites Everywhere

Meteorites small and large have probably fallen unnoticed almost everywhere on Earth. Thinly populated areas, such as Australia and the Antarctic, are popular hunting grounds for meteorites because the meteorites remain undisturbed.

The impact of a large meteorite generally makes a deep impression, called a crater, on Earth's surface. The most recent large meteorite, with a crater about 4,200 feet (1,270 km) across and 600 feet (180 m) deep, fell some 25,000 years ago near Winslow, Arizona. The crater is open to visitors. The largest known meteorite, the Hoba West meteorite in Namibia, Africa, weighs an estimated 66 tons (60 metric tons). It still lies where it fell.

Most meteorites weigh in around 2 pounds (1 kg). They may drop to Earth in a shower, the result of a larger meteorite breaking up in the atmosphere. A number of meteorites, called SNC types (S, N, and C are the initial letters of three towns—one each in India, France, and Egypt—where they were first noted), may have resulted from collisions on the Moon or Mars. Most natural history museums have meteorites on display.

Do all meteors come from comets?

Not all meteors come from comets. The word "meteor" specifies a space object that enters Earth's atmosphere, but burns up before hitting the planet's surface. They can come from anywhere in space, since meteors are simply debris. The solar system is full of chunks of rock and metal, left over from the creation of the planets and various collisions, as well as burned-out or broken-up comets.

What are meteorites?

Meteorites are not the same as meteors; but meteors can become meteorites. Meteorites are generally small chunks of rock (stone or metal matter), many from asteroids, that enter Earth's atmosphere and hit the planet's surface.

Meteorite Life

In September 1969, a meteorite fell to the Earth near Murchison, Australia, north of Melbourne. It was rapidly taken to a laboratory, which prevented it from being contaminated by terrestrial matter. This meant that scientists could claim that what they discovered on it came from outer space, not Earth. They found sixteen different amino acids, which form protein; various nucleic acids, which carry genetic information; and chemicals similar to the structural elements of living cells. In other words, scientists discovered evidence of the building blocks of life that didn't originate on Earth. The meteorite was dated back 4.5 billion years, right around the time of Earth's formation.

What are meteorites made of?

These rocks from outer space come in three basic groups (although there are many subgroups): stony, iron, and stony-iron. In general, stony meteorites resemble material from Earth's crust. Iron meteorites are almost pure iron and nickel—90 percent iron and 10 percent nickel—the same metals that are believed to make up Earth's core. Stony-iron meteorites contain both types of material. Meteorites all date back about 4.6 billion years, so it is safe to assume that they contain original matter that made the solar system. A subgroup of stony meteorites, known as carbonaceous chondrites, also contain carbon and amino acids—two building blocks of life. The Murchison meteorite, which fell in Australia in 1969, was a carbonaceous chondrite.

In more recent scientific terminology, stony meteorites are called aerolites; stony-iron are known as siderolites; and iron are termed siderites.

Are meteorites dangerous?

Meteorites can fall anywhere on Earth. Depending on where they fall and their size, they could cause considerable damage. But this has rarely happened. Most meteorites weigh only 2.2 pounds (1 kg), and most break into smaller pieces or vaporize on impact. The most destructive meteorite of all time is purely hypothetical: Many scientists believe that a huge meteorite (maybe a comet or an asteroid) struck Earth some 65 million years ago, causing the extinction of the dinosaurs.

The second largest meteorite, the Ahnighito (37.5 tons [34 metric tons]), fell in Greenland and for centuries supplied local inhabitants with iron for tools and weapons; the explorer Robert Peary bought the Ahnighito and, in 1897, sold it to the American Museum of Natural History in New York City.

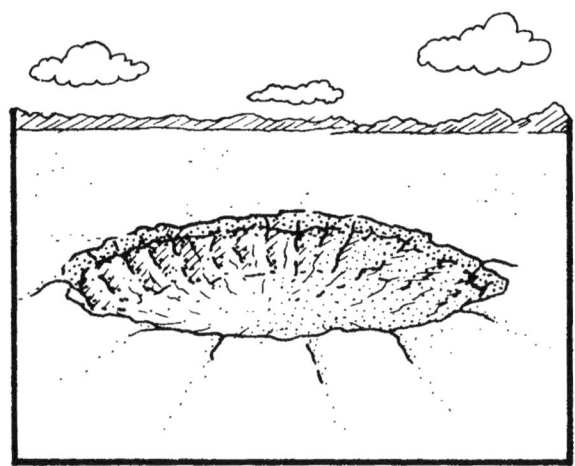

Will a meteorite hit Earth again?

Meteorites hit Earth every day, but are so small that only a handful each year are noticed. Chances are about a million to one that a substantial meteorite will reach Earth in any given year, but, statistically, it is inevitable.

What is a planet?

Many qualities define a planet, but not all planets meet all criteria. A planet is a body that revolves around a star. It does not generate light, but reflects the light of a star. While stars appear as points of light through a telescope, planets look like disks.

What are the differences between planets and stars?

The elements that make up stars—mostly hydrogen and helium—are also found on planets. Jupiter, Saturn, and Uranus's atmospheres, for example, are also mostly hydrogen and helium. Earth's matter is mostly carbon-based, and carbon is found in stars, particularly old-age white dwarfs. Stars, however, grow big enough to spark nuclear fusion and planets don't. Consequently, planets do not shine with their own light, but reflect the light of a local star, and are cooler than stars. Planets "wander" across the sky, meaning that while stars are steadfast in relation to each other, planets appear to travel through the constellations. Planets are less massive and dense than stars. Orbiting asteroids meet some of the criteria for planets, which is why they are sometimes called minor planets.

The word planet *comes from the Greek word for wanderer.*

When did the planets form?

We know that Earth came into existence about 4.6 billion years ago, and it is most likely that the other planets formed at about the same time, just after the Sun started shining some 5 billion years ago.

Almost all meteorites date to around this same time, which substantiates this theory of when the planets and solar system began. Of course, one could say that the solar system began, as did everything, with the big bang, the theoretical burst (not really an explosion) that created the universe. But the planets, as we see them now, probably came into existence 4.5 to 5 billion years ago.

How does a planet form?

Scientists have come up with many different theories about planet formation. The protoplanet theory, summarized here, seems to answer the most questions without raising too many others.

When a star bursts into existence, its released energy shoots some gases, dust, and particles outward into rotation around itself. While the matter spins in eddies, or little cyclones, gravity causes particles to collide and join, forming **planetesimals**—bodies of planetary matter

Planet Chart

Name	Rotation period (days.hours.mins.secs)	Orbital period (days/years)	Orbital speed (miles/km per sec.)	Inclination
Mercury	58.6d	87.97d	30/48	7.00°
Venus	243.0d	224.7d	22/35	3.39°
Earth	23h.56m.4s	365.25d	18.5/30	0°
Mars	24h.37m.26s	687d	15/24	1.85°
Jupiter	9h.55m.30s	11.86y	8.1/13.1	1.30°
Saturn	10h.13m.59s	29.46y	6/9.64	2.49°
Uranus	17h.4m	84.01y	4.2/6.8	0.77°
Neptune	16h.7m	164.79y	3.4/5.4	1.77°
Pluto	6h.9m.12s	247.69y	2.9/4.7	17.2°

Name	Temperature (F°/C°)	Gravity force (% or X Earth)	Escape velocity (miles/km per second)
Mercury	−270 to 800/−167 to 427	38%	2.7/4.3
Venus	882/472	91%	6.4/10.3
Earth	−60 to 120/−51 to 48	100%	6.9/11.2
Mars	−190 to −22/−123 to −30	38%	3.1/5.0
Jupiter	−180/−117	2.54×	37.0/60.0
Saturn	−292/−180	1.16×	22.1/35.6
Uranus	−366/−221	91%	13.0/21.0
Neptune	−357/−216	1.2×	14.9/24.0
Pluto	−382/−230	6%	0.75/1.2

Name	Satellites	Special Features
Mercury	0	Hottest planet; atmosphere of solar wind
Venus	0	Retrograde rotation; close to Earth's mass
Earth	1	Only planet to support life
Mars	2	Red, cratered planet
Jupiter	16	Largest planet; Great Red Spot; ring system
Saturn	18	Prominent ring system
Uranus	15	Extreme axial tilt; ring system
Neptune	8	Equatorial winds blow retrograde to rotation; ring system
Pluto	1	Smallest planet; orbit crosses Neptune's orbit

about 6 miles (10 km) in diameter. The planetesimals continue to attract matter and other planetesimals, which accrete (join) to form larger planetary bodies called protoplanets. Finally, the protoplanet exhausts most of the material within reach and settles into orbit as a full-fledged planet.

The hypothetical process of planet formation could be said to start with the big bang, as did everything. A nebula—a cloud of gases and dust that amassed as a result of the big bang—formed some 10 billion years ago right here, where the solar system exists. The nebula contracted until it exploded into the Sun, about 5 billion years ago. From there, so the hypothesis goes, the planets we know began their formation.

Why do the planets rotate around the Sun?

The powerful gravity of the Sun keeps the planets in regular orbit. Even before the planets were born, the matter that created them rotated and spun around the Sun, then kept spinning as a result of the Sun's explosion into existence. If it weren't for gravity, the material would have gone sailing out into space forever. Instead, the matter accreted into the nine known planets, which continue to rotate around the Sun.

Are there planets in other solar systems?

There is no sure answer to this question. Some scientists believe that other planets exist in solar systems around all other stars. If you take the view that planets are simply leftover spinning matter from the formation of a star, why not? But we do not have hard evidence of any other planets or solar systems.

Why are some planets mostly gas?

When the sun began its nuclear energy production, the explosion sent gases, dust, and particles flying outward. The lightest matter—such as the gases hydrogen and helium—simply flew farther away. The farther reaches from the Sun were not effected as much by the Sun's heat, so the gases remained relatively inert (they didn't change into other, heavier forms).

This matter formed the outer planets, or **gas giants**, as they are also known. Heavier material, which didn't travel so far—and so reacted in part to the higher temperatures nearer the Sun—helped to create the inner planets, also known as the **terrestrial**, or earthlike, **planets**.

Planet Names in Mythology

Mercury

Mercury was the fleet-footed protector of merchants and travelers, as well as Jupiter's messenger.

Venus

The Roman goddess of love, Venus was prone to fits of anger and jealousy. She once caused all the women of one island to stink so much that their husbands abandoned them.

Mars

Mars, the Roman god of war and agriculture, fathered Romulus and Remus, the mythical founders of Rome.

Jupiter

Jupiter was the flamboyant Roman king of the gods and goddesses. It seems right, therefore, that the largest planet is named for him.

Saturn

Saturn was a Titan (Titans preceded the gods) dethroned by Jupiter. He was sometimes associated with the underworld and, at the end of the year, his festival inverted social order: slaves ruled masters and waiters were waited upon.

Uranus

Uranus was an ancient god, even to the Romans. He is credited with bringing civilization and culture to the world, and was himself a great astronomer.

Neptune

The Roman god Neptune ruled over the seas, lakes, ponds, and springs. He was known to dry up rivers when he was angry. One of the most powerful gods, Neptune also had the greatest number of children.

Pluto

Also known as Hades, Pluto was the sinister god of the dead and the underworld. Hades's name meant "the invisible," and was rarely spoken out loud. He was usually called Pluton, or Pluto, which meant "the rich." Pluto seems an appropriate name for this little understood, but tantalizing, planet.

What is a planet's elliptical orbit?

Ellipses are oval shapes. All planets orbit the Sun in ellipses, not circles. Some ellipses are nearly flat, while others are almost circular. A planet's **aphelion** is the point in its elliptical orbit when it is farthest from the Sun; its **perihelion** is its closest point to the Sun. A planet moves faster at its perihelion than at its aphelion. When

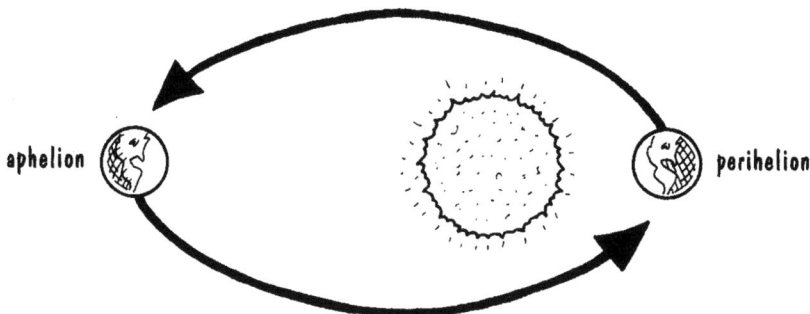

Aphelion and perihelion are, respectively, a planetary orbit's farthest and nearest points to the Sun. All planets' orbits are elliptical (flattened circles) and the Sun is not in the exact center of any orbit. When we say the Sun is the center of the solar system, we are not speaking in terms of precise location.

we mention the distance or speed of a planet's orbit, we are referring to the average, unless otherwise specified.

What is a planet's orbital plane?

A planet's orbital plane is the flat surface along which it orbits the Sun. If you sliced an orange in half and put the halves back together with an oval piece of cardboard in between, the orange could represent the Sun and the cardboard could represent a planet's orbit. The planet would follow the edge of the oval, never traveling above or below it. If you sliced the orange at another angle and fit another oval of cardboard in between the halves, that cardboard would represent a different orbital plane. Every planet orbits the Sun on a different orbital plane.

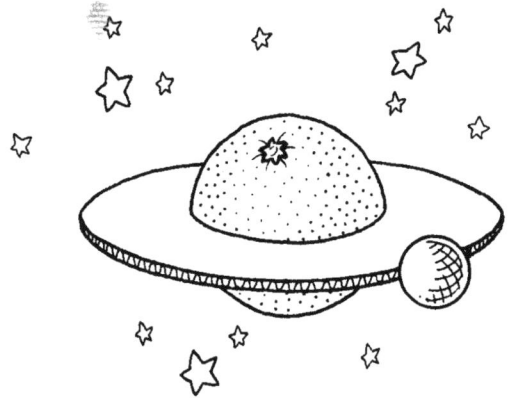

Orbital Patterns

There are three basic solar orbits: elliptical, parabolic, and hyperbolic. Planets have elliptical orbits, bound by the force of the Sun's gravity. Elliptical orbits can be anywhere between almost circular and almost flat ovals. If the speed of an object is equal to the Sun's escape velocity, 380 miles (630 km) per second, it will have a parabolic orbit. It will swing in a relatively narrow arc around the Sun and then fly off into space. An object with even greater speed than escape velocity will have a hyperbolic orbit. Its arc around the Sun will be wide and then it, too, will fly off into space.

What is orbital tilt?

Every planet orbits the Sun on a different plane. The differences between orbital planes are measured by their angles to Earth's orbital plane. The difference is known as **orbital tilt** or **incline**. For instance, Mars's orbit is tilted at an angle of 1.85° to Earth's orbital plane. Orbital plane inclines range from 0.77° (Uranus) to 17.2° (Pluto). If the planets all existed on the same orbital plane, there'd be massive pileups on the heavenly highways!

What are inferior and superior planets?

Although these terms sound judgmental, they are not meant that way. Relative to a particular planet, **inferior planets** are those that are closer to the Sun and **superior planets** are ones that are farther away from the Sun. For Earth, Mercury and Venus are inferior planets and all the others are superior planets. For Uranus, Neptune and Pluto are superior planets and all the rest are inferior planets.

What is syzygy?

This bizarre-looking word, pronounced **sih**-zih-gee, is the alignment of three celestial bodies in a row. For instance, during a lunar or solar eclipse, the Sun, Earth, and Moon are in syzygy.

What are inferior and superior conjunctions?

These terms refer specifically to the alignment of the Sun, Earth, and either of the inferior planets (Mercury and Venus). At some point, all three line up in a row, sometimes with the Sun in the middle and sometimes with the inferior planet in the middle. When the Sun is in the middle, the inferior planet is at **superior conjunction** and can't be seen from Earth. When the inferior planet is in the middle, it is at **inferior conjunction**.

What is opposition?

This is the term for syzygy (alignment) of the Sun, Earth, and a superior planet when Earth is in the middle. This places the superior planet in full sunlight, making it best for viewing. A **favorable opposition** occurs when the superior planet is at its closest to the Sun (perihelion). An **unfavorable opposition** is when the alignment takes place at the superior planet's farthest distance from the Sun (aphelion). Favorable and unfavorable oppositions are fancy ways of saying a closer object is easier to see—and study—than one farther away.

What is a transit?

A **transit** occurs when a smaller celestial object passes in front of a larger one. For instance, all inferior planets will cross the face of the Sun at some point in their orbits. When Mercury transits the Sun, as seen from Earth, the planet may be seen as a dark spot traveling across the Sun's surface.

What is occultation?

An **occultation** occurs when any celestial body obscures the sight of another by passing in front of it. The word is applied to stars, planets, asteroids, comets, and all other space objects.

What are the minor planets?

In the **asteroid belt**, between the planets Mars and Jupiter, a band of **asteroids**—relatively small, irregular, rocky chunks of matter—orbits the Sun. They are also called **minor planets**.

How many minor planets exist?

More than 5,000 minor planets (orbiting asteroids) have been cataloged since 1801, when the largest, numbered 1 and named Ceres (1 Ceres), was sighted by Italian astronomer Giuseppe Piazzi. Some 200 more are discov-

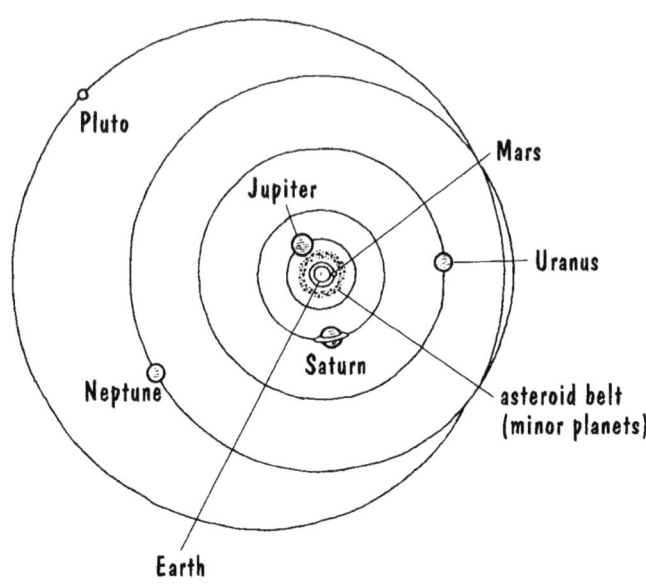

Pluto

Mars

Jupiter

Uranus

Neptune

Saturn

asteroid belt
(minor planets)

Earth

The asteroid belt, filled with about 5,000 asteroids, lies between the orbits of Jupiter and Mars. The combined mass of all the asteroids is less than one-thousandth that of Earth. That fact, and the gravitational battle between Jupiter and Mars, may help to explain why the asteroids never formed a planet.

ered every year. Astronomers estimate that 50 percent of all asteroids that are 6 miles (1 km) or larger in diameter have been identified, including about 99 percent of all large asteroids (over 60 miles [100 km] across).

Where did minor planets come from?

The materials found in the minor planets are similar to those of the major planets. Most meteorites found on Earth are asteroids, composed of the same rocky-metallic materials as planets. Their existence supports eighteenth-century astronomer Johann Titius's theory that there should have been another major planet. Titius developed a remarkably accurate mathematical calculation to explain the spacing between the planets—except that there was one planet missing, right where the asteroid belt is located.

Trojan asteroids, which reside in Jupiter's orbit rather than the asteroid belt, are made of the same stuff as

Jupiter. They probably were created by pieces of Jupiter's core breaking off during formative collisions.

What are minor-planet asteroids made of?

There are three basic types of these asteroids, based on their physical composition. The rather common C-type asteroids are made mostly of carbon-based matter. They do not reflect much sunlight. S-type asteroids contain metals and silica minerals. They are brighter than C-type asteroids, but not as bright as M-type asteroids. M-type asteroids seem to be made primarily of metals and are highly reflective.

The minor planets sometimes seem remarkably familiar. Radar has tentatively detected the presence of water on the largest and brightest asteroid, named Ceres. A thin layer of soil covers the cratered surface of Gaspra, the first asteroid to be photographed close-up by a spacecraft.

How big are the minor planets?

The size of these asteroids varies from tiny particles of dust to the minor planet Ceres, about 625 miles (1,000 km) in diameter. Combined, however, the estimated mass of all asteroids comes to less than one-thousandth that of Earth.

How were the minor planets discovered?

Late in the eighteenth century, a mathematical equation, now called the Titius-Bode law, was formalized to figure out the distance between major planets. It worked like this:

Planet	Exponential Factor of 3	Add 4	Divide by 10	Answer	Distance From Sun (AU)
Mercury	0	+ 4	divided by 10	= 0.40	0.39
Venus	3	+ 4	divided by 10	= 0.70	0.72
Earth	6	+ 4	divided by 10	= 1.00	1.00
Mars	12	+ 4	divided by 10	= 1.60	1.52
???	24	+ 4	divided by 10	= 2.80	
Jupiter	48	+ 4	divided by 10	= 5.20	5.20
Saturn	96	+ 4	divided by 10	= 10.00	9.54
Uranus	192	+ 4	divided by 10	= 19.60	19.20

Planetary Plagiarism?

Johann Bode published Johann Titius's planetary spacing equation in 1772—8 years after Titius worked it out—as his own. It was known as Bode's law until Bode admitted his plagiarism in 1826, when it became known as the Titius-Bode law.

This equation shows a remarkably accurate prediction of planets' distance from the Sun. (In fact, Uranus was discovered after the equation was published, right where it should have been.) Between Mars and Jupiter, a planet seemed to be missing, so scientists went looking for it and found Ceres, and then the rest of the asteroid belt.

The discovery of Neptune and Pluto, however, proved that the Titius-Bode law was nothing more than a mathematical oddity. According to the law, Neptune should have been 38.8 AUs from the sun; it is 30. Pluto should be 77.2 AUs, but it is only 39. While the Titius-Bode law is no longer considered accurate, it was useful for a time.

Earth and its Moon

What is Earth like compared to other planets?

We are all well acquainted with Earth, but try to think about Earth in the same way you think about the other planets. Earth is the third planet from the Sun, and it orbits in a near-circular ellipse. The planet is about the same size as Venus, and it has the same mass and density, but the similarities stop there. Most of Earth's surface is covered by water (70 percent), and the landmasses appear to have once been joined. Active volcanoes and earthquakes are in evidence. Earth has one satellite. Perhaps the most interesting feature of this planet is the presence of life.

What is Earth made of?

Earth is a rocky planet that geologists divide into three layers: the core, the mantle, and the crust. The core, about 4,000 miles (6,700 km) in diameter, is believed to be a solid sphere of iron (90 percent) and nickel (10 percent). Recent observations seem to indicate that the core is made of an inner and outer layer rotating at different speeds. Every 111 years, the inner core completes an additional rotation. Around the core lies the mantle. It is composed of dense rock, partially molten (melted). The molten rock is active, moving around within the 1,000-mile-thick (1,700-km-thick) mantle. We are familiar with the crust—a thin layer of rock and soil—because it is the

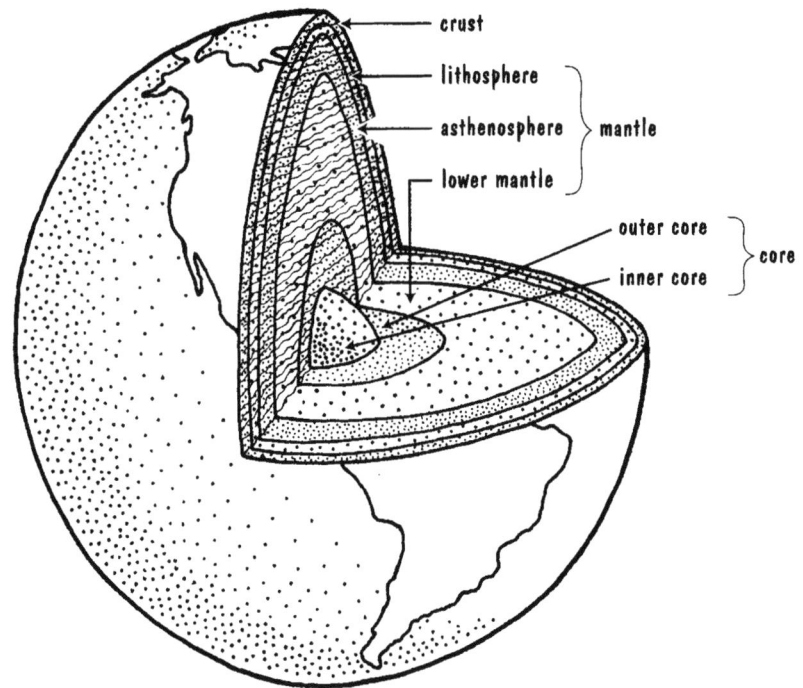

crust
lithosphere
asthenosphere } mantle
lower mantle
outer core
inner core } core

Earth's core is made of iron and nickel, some of it molten. The mantle is dense rock, some solid and some molten. Molten rock in the mantle is called magma. If it escapes to the surface, it becomes known as lava. Rocky materials make up Earth's thin crust.

surface on which we live. At its deepest, the crust extends only about 40 miles (65 km) down to the mantle.

Why is most of Earth's surface underwater?

Earth began, like the other terrestrial planets, as a very hot mass of volcanic material from the newly formed Sun. The volcanoes released water vapor, which rose, cooled, and formed clouds, which precipitated. The rain hastened the general cooling of the planet until Earth was cool enough that the water began pooling. After billions of years, water covered the entire planet.

How did Earth develop land?

Volcanic activity led to the creation of land. Lava that spewed up during eruptions cooled to form first thin layers of the rock called basalt. In time, the layers grew to become the foundations of the landmasses. Chemical reactions between the volcanic materials, the water, and the atmosphere—everything continued to evolve simultaneously—eventually built up a diversity of rock that became the continents.

How did life appear on Earth?

No one knows for sure, but somehow the elements and chemicals on Earth developed into single living cells. These cells ate, reproduced, and died, leaving behind more material from which to make new life. The single plant cells evolved into single animal cells, which not only ate, reproduced, and died, but found ways to move around. From there the process continued until we wound up with people, New York City, video games, and spacecraft. For a more detailed answer, check your local library for the thousands of books and articles debating this hot topic.

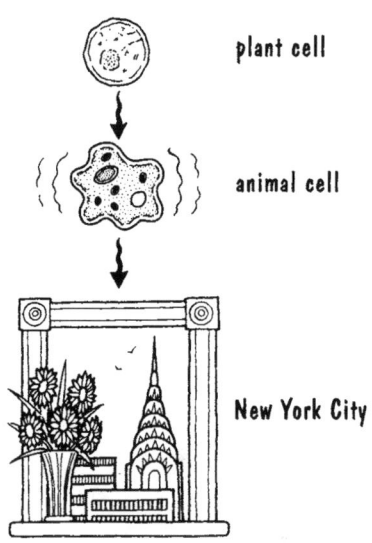

plant cell

animal cell

New York City

Does Earth have an atmosphere?

Earth does have an atmosphere, and it is segmented into layers. The **troposphere** begins at the planet's surface and extends between 6 (10 km) and 10 miles (16 km) high. Above that, the **stratosphere** reaches 30 miles (50 km) from Earth's surface. The next 20 miles (33 km) is called the **mesosphere**, and after that comes the **thermosphere,** which stretches up 400 miles (600 km) into the atmosphere. After the thermosphere comes outer space, which we call the **exosphere**.

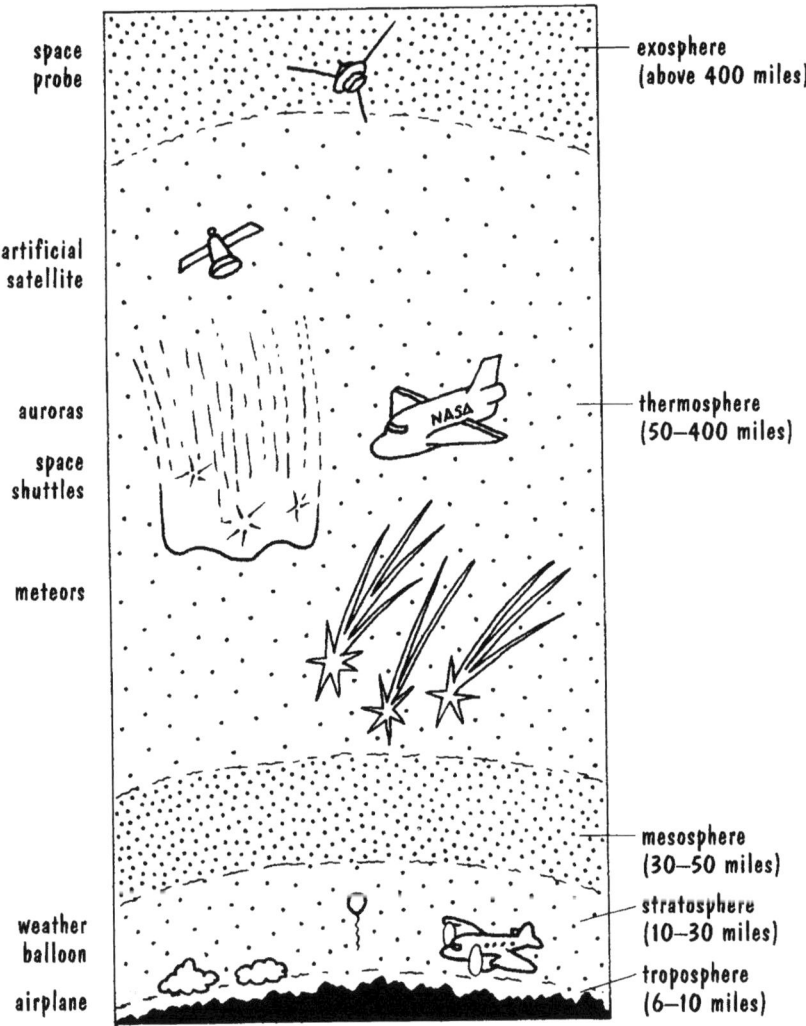

space
probe

exosphere
(above 400 miles)

artificial
satellite

auroras

thermosphere
(50–400 miles)

space
shuttles

meteors

mesosphere
(30–50 miles)

stratosphere
(10–30 miles)

weather
balloon

troposphere
(6–10 miles)

airplane

Layers of Earth's Atmosphere

Why does Earth have an atmosphere?

The gravitational force of Earth is sufficient to trap gases and particles around the planet. Without this gravity, the atmosphere would never have formed, as its components would have gone flying off into space.

What is the troposphere like?

The troposphere is the atmosphere we breathe. It consists mostly of nitrogen (78 percent) and oxygen (21 percent), with trace amounts of ten other elements. Water vapor can account for up to 4 percent of the air, depending on the climate. All weather occurs within the troposphere, though cumulonimbus clouds can poke through to the next layer. In the troposphere, temperatures decline the higher you go until you reach about 6.5 miles (11 km). The temperature at the top of the troposphere is about −76°F (−60°C).

What is the stratosphere like?

The upper part of the stratosphere contains ozone, a gas that absorbs ultraviolet rays from the Sun. This heats up the stratosphere from about −67°F (−55°C) to 32°F (0°C).

What is ozone?

The ozone in the stratosphere is a unique form of oxygen. It acts as a powerful barrier against the Sun's strong and dangerous ultraviolet rays. Without the ozone layer, ultraviolet radiation could cause many health problems for humans—from skin irritation to cancer—not to mention harm to all other life.

What is the ozone hole?

A break, or hole, in the ozone layer exists over the southern polar region of Earth. This hole allows ultraviolet light from the Sun to reach Earth undiluted by ozone. There is disagreement over whether this hole is a natural phenomenon or the result of man-made pollutants.

What is the mesosphere like?

By the time you reach the mesosphere there is only one-thousandth the amount of breathable air as when you are at sea level. The temperatures again begin to fall, plummeting to −130°F (−90°C).

What is the thermosphere like?

Temperatures rise again in the thermosphere because of the presence of gas and particles that absorb the Sun's rays. In fact, the temperature reaches well above 212°F (100°C), the boiling point of water.

What is the ionosphere?

This layer of the atmosphere overlaps the mesosphere and thermosphere. In the **ionosphere**, some molecules become electrically charged, which enables them to reflect radio waves back and forth to Earth in radio communication.

What is the exosphere like?

The molecules in the exosphere are so thinly dispersed that they have as good a chance of escaping the atmosphere as colliding with another molecule. When nonscientists talk about "outer space," they are actually describing the exosphere.

What is Earth's magnetosphere?

Earth has a natural electromagnetic field of charged particles. These particles essentially allow for the existence of natural electricity. The particles reside in a layer around Earth called the **magnetosphere**. It is shaped like a teardrop as a result of the solar wind pushing the bulk of it away from the Sun. The area on the side facing the Sun extends for about 40,000 miles (65,000 km). The other side reaches out beyond the distance to the Moon, 231,000 miles (380,000 km).

What is a satellite?

A **satellite** is an object that orbits another, parent, object. For instance, the Moon is Earth's satellite. Earth is a satellite of the Sun. The solar system is a satellite of the Milky Way's nucleus. All planets, except for Mercury and Venus, have at least one satellite, or moon. Earth has one: the Moon. Nowadays some satellites are fabricated, such as space stations.

How did Earth get its satellite?

There are many theories about how this happened. The current favorite says that a huge asteroid—maybe the same one that is thought to have tilted Earth's axis—hit Earth, throwing off a mass of debris into a broken ring around the planet. Over time, the debris coalesced, creating the Moon. At first the Moon was much closer to

Earth, but it gradually settled in the orbit it has today.

What is the "sister theory" of the Moon's creation?

The sister theory holds that the Moon may have formed along with Earth as a result of the formation of the solar system. When astronauts retrieved moon rocks in 1969, however, scientists discovered that they were not made of matter from the solar nebula. If they were, they would have matched Earth rocks more closely. Moon rocks contain material such as that found in Earth's crust, which supports the theory of an asteroid collision.

Why does the Moon appear to be smaller when it's higher in the sky?

The Moon doesn't actually get smaller as it rises. It's an optical illusion (a trick that's played on our eyesight). When we see the Moon on Earth's horizon, our brain registers its size in comparison to objects on Earth: buildings, trees, the ocean. It appears huge. As it rises, our brain loses its earthbound scale of reference. The Moon seems to grow smaller. This phenomenon is known as the Moon illusion.

The Man in the Moon

We've almost all seen him, the Man in the Moon. His bright, benign face shines down on Earth around the time of the full moon. But he isn't really there. This demonstration will show you what is going on.

Equipment

approximately seven dominoes (or matchboxes, or any small objects you can make stand upright on a table)
flashlight

1. Set up the dominoes on a table in the shape of a face: two eyes, a nose, and a mouth.
2. Darken the room. Shine the flashlight on the dominoes from above and at an angle. Watch the shadows on the table form an eerie face.

The surface of the Moon has mountains, ridges, and craters, which cast shadows when the Sun's light hits them. They seem to make a face because people tend to see familiar objects in random shapes, just as when we look at clouds, we can see ships, monsters, and castles.

How does the Moon affect Earth?

The Moon's gravity creates tides. As Earth rotates on its axis, different parts of the world face the Moon. The

*The mean dis-
tance of the
Moon from Earth
is 230,000 miles
(384,000 km).*

waters in those areas are attracted to the Moon because of the satellite's gravitational pull. While the Moon passes overhead, water in oceans and large lakes follows it, creating high tides (higher water level) closer to the Moon and low tides (lower water level) where water has left to go chasing after the Moon. The Moon's gravity creates land tides as well as water tides. Earth's surface actually rises and falls as much as 1 or 2 inches (2.5 to 5 cm) when the Moon passes over it.

The Moon's gravity could, but does not, create tides by itself. The Sun helps. If there were no Moon, the Sun's gravity would still be enough to cause tides, though they would not be as large.

What causes the phases of the Moon?

The Moon reflects the light the Sun shines on it. The apparent changes in its shape—from full to gibbous to half to crescent to new—does not mean the Moon is actually getting smaller or larger. The Moon appears to wane (grow smaller) and wax (grow larger) because, as it rotates around Earth, we can only see those sections that receive sunlight.

*It takes the
Moon about
29.5 days to go
from one new
moon to the
next.*

Remember that we can only see one side of the Moon from Earth. The far side of the Moon is always hidden from us. When the Moon's orbit places it between Earth and the Sun, the Sun is shining only on the side we can't see, so we experience a new moon. Halfway through its orbit, the Moon is on the other side of Earth from the Sun, and we see a full moon. In between the new and full moons, we see a waxing or new crescent, then a half moon called the first quarter (14 days after new and full moons), then a waxing or new gibbous until the full moon. After a full moon, we see a waning or old crescent, half moon (also called last quarter) and an old or waxing gibbous leading to the full moon.

Why do the phases take longer than one Moon orbit?

For the phases to begin over again, the Moon, Earth, and Sun all have to line up in a row (whether you start a phase at a new moon or a full moon). While one revolu-

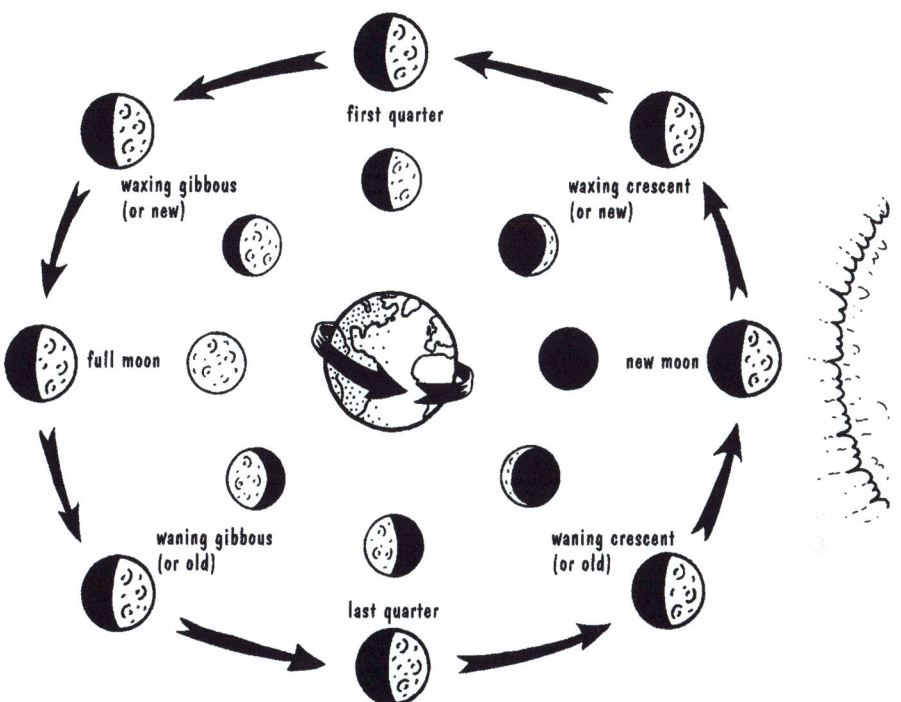

We see phases of the Moon because as the Moon orbits Earth, its shadow is thrown onto the surface of the planet. The inner ring of moons shows what the Moon looks like from Earth.

tion of the Moon around Earth lines up the Moon and Earth again, the Sun is no longer in the same place. This is because at the same time the Moon is orbiting Earth, the Earth–Moon system (the phrase used to describe Earth and its satellite as one unit, because they are relatively close to each other) is orbiting the Sun. The Earth–Moon system travels approximately 3.5 million miles (5.8 million km) around the Sun, at a speed of 66,600 miles (111,000 km) per hour. It takes about two more days (orbit: 27.3 days; phase cycle: 29.5 days) for the Moon, Earth, and Sun to line up again.

The Moon makes one revolution around Earth every 27.3 days.

What is a lunar eclipse?

When the Moon, Earth, and the Sun line up so that the planet is between the satellite and the star, the Sun's light is blocked from reaching the Moon by Earth.

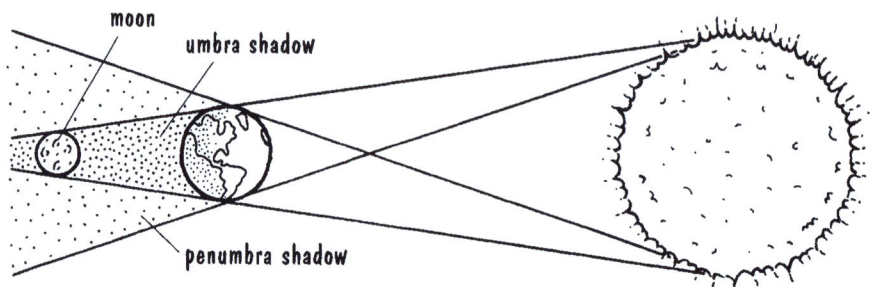

A lunar eclipse requires that the Sun, Earth, and Moon be lined up with Earth in the middle. Earth's shadow causes the Moon to disappear from view—either entirely (in the area of the umbra on Earth) or partially (as seen from Earth's surface, labeled penumbra).

Essentially, the Moon is in the shadow—umbra or penumbra—of Earth. People living in the umbra experience "night." The Moon seems to have vanished in a total **lunar eclipse**. A partial eclipse occurs when the Moon enters only part of Earth's shadow, or penumbra.

What do we know about the Moon's interior?

Seismographic instruments placed on the Moon by the Apollo astronauts determined that the satellite is mostly solid, with a crust, mantle, and core. Scientists are not sure what the core is made of, or whether it is at least partially molten (melted). We do know, however, that it is made of the Moon's densest elements and is about 800 miles (1,400 km) in diameter. Solid rock makes up the mantle, some 600 miles (1,000 km) deep. The hard, rocky crust is about 40 miles (60 km) thick on the side that faces Earth, and is thicker on the far side.

The Straight Wall on the Moon

Neither straight, nor a wall, the Straight Wall is a fascinating topographical feature in the Moon's southwest quadrant on the eastern border of the Mare Nubium. It *looks* like a straight, precise wall, but it is a fault, or geological crack in the surface, with a 1,000-foot (300-m) drop on its west side. Because of the angle of the sun hitting the drop-off, the fault appears as a black line before the full moon. Right after the full moon, however, the Straight Wall gleams brilliantly.

What is the Moon's surface made of?

When astronauts on the Apollo space missions (1969–1972) brought moon rocks back to Earth, scientists were able to answer this question for the first time. (The answer was not green cheese!) The Moon's crust is made of rock very similar to terrestrial volcanic rock, but with less iron and potassium and more titanium. The surface is covered by an inch or so (a few centimeters) of powdered rock called regolith. This dust was made by meteorites and micrometeorites shattering the Moon's surface.

Why do we see so much detail on the Moon?

The Moon is relatively close to Earth, and so it is the most obvious object in the sky, aside from the Sun. It is also huge for a satellite: one-quarter the size of Earth. The Moon's gravity is not strong enough to hold an atmosphere, so there are no winds to fill the **craters** and crevices with dust. There is no wind, and no proof of water, to erode mountains. Without water, the Moon has no lakes to hide ground formations or vegetation to obscure its contours. Almost every detail is visible.

What is the Moon's landscape like?

The Moon has highlands and lowlands. The main feature on the Moon's surface are the hundreds of thousands of craters, or the remnants of craters, found in both regions, some with crater **rays** of ejected lunar material emanating out from their edges. Besides craters, there are mountains, mares, rills, and domes.

We always see the same side of the Moon from Earth because the Moon rotates around its axis once and orbits Earth once in the same period of time: 27.3 days.

What is the difference between the lunar highlands and lowlands?

The highlands are areas of mountains and valleys, whereas the lowlands are dominated by mares, or areas of flat plains. Craters are found in both highlands and lowlands. The side of the Moon we see from Earth is split 50/50 between the two terrains. The side we can't see is almost all highland.

Why are there so many craters on the Moon?

There are hundred of thousands of craters visible on the Moon, measuring from a few feet (meters) across (craterlets) to about 150 miles (240 km) across (basins or walled plains).

The craters seem to be the result of both meteorites and volcanic activity. Most scientists agree that the Moon

Major Visible Lunar Craters

Name	Diameter	Quadrant	Other Features
Arago	17 miles (29 km)	NE	Nearby collection of domes with craterlets
Ariadeus	9 miles (15 km)	NE	150-mile (250-km) branched rill
Aristarchus	22 miles (37 km)	NW	Brightest crater on the Moon
Bailly	176 miles (294 km)	SW	Largest crater
Clavius	139 miles (232 km)	SW	13,000-foot (4,000-m) walls; arced crater chain on floor
Grimaldi	116 miles (193 km)	SW	8,000-foot (2,500-m) walls; darkest feature on the moon
Petavius	102 miles (170 km)	SE	11,500-foot (3,500-m) walls; central mountain range
Schickard	121 miles (202 km)	SW	Low walls; hills and craterlets on floor
Schiller	108 miles (180 km)	SW	Two connected craters
Taruntius	36 miles (60 km)	NE	Concentric inner crater rim; great central peak
Tycho	50 miles (84 km)	SE	The Great Ray Crater; bright rays streak from its walls

came under a meteorite bombardment some 4.5 billion years ago, shortly after it was formed. Within 1 billion years, the meteorites abruptly stopped. The Moon's interior rapidly increased in temperature, causing massive volcanic eruptions. While the volcanoes distorted many of the meteoric craters, they created craters of their own.

How does a meteorite make a lunar crater?

A lunar crater is not simply a large hole in the ground. Meteorites build up energy as well as speed. This energy has the force of dynamite upon impact, causing the meteorite and the surrounding crust to vaporize. Material that isn't instantly incinerated is thrown out of the crater. The ejected debris creates walls around the crater's rim anywhere from just a few feet (meters) to a few miles (kilometers) high. The energy sends shock waves into the surface, causing moonquakes. Part of the rim may fall back into the crater, which is why some craters have terraced walls. Where the meteorite's impact was greatest, the crust may rebound and form a peak in the center of the crater.

Moon Erosion

Though the era of massive meteorite bombardment has been over for some 3.5 billion years, the Moon is constantly hit by micrometeorites. (*Micro* means tiny, and meteorites are matter from space that crash into the surface of a planet or satellite.) Micrometeorites are celestial debris—remnants of asteroids, comets, and planets—that hit the Moon at speeds of up to 70,000 miles (113,000 km) per hour. While these tiny particles of rock and metal cause erosion, it takes about a million years for them to alter even 0.04 inches (1 mm) of the surface.

What are crater rays?

Sometimes called rays and sometimes called streaks, crater rays are visible lines that radiate from the center or rims of some craters. Rays are made up of material that was ejected from the crater when a meteorite hit the lunar surface. The crater Tycho, located in the southeast quadrant of the Moon, illustrates the most spectacular example of crater rays.

Are the lunar mountains like mountains on Earth?

Lunar mountains bear little resemblance to mountains on Earth. They were not formed by plate tectonics, as on Earth, but mostly border the mares and craters. About the only thing they have in common is height, and in that category, the Moon beats out Earth: Several peaks in the Moon's Leibnitz Range are taller than Mt. Everest, the tallest mountain on Earth, over 29,000 feet (8,000 meters).

Earthlings have given lunar mountain ranges such familiar terrestrial names as Alps, Caucasus, Pyrenees, and Urals.

What are mares like?

Galileo first named the dark areas of the Moon mares (or **maria**) after the Latin word *mare*, which means "sea." They looked like large oceans, and that's what they were thought to be until the twentieth century. We now know that mares are large, relatively flat plains of lava hardened into basalt. Oddly enough, they are connected in much the same way Earth's oceans are, but that's as far as the similarity goes. They carry such fancy names as the Sea of Tranquility, the Lake of Dreamers, the Bay of Rainbows, and the Marsh of Decay. The names have no scientific or descriptive meaning.

What is a rill?

Rills are extended crevices on the Moon's surface. They can run up to at least 150 miles (250 km) and over a mile (1.6 km) wide. The thousands of rills that cut through the Moon's terrain were probably formed from channels of molten lava.

What are lunar domes?

Lunar domes, so named for their shape, may be the remnants of volcanic vents, or openings. They are like volcanic bubbles or blisters dotting the landscape of the mares. Domes measure up to 6 miles (10 km) in diameter.

How do the near and far sides of the Moon differ?

One unexpected difference is that there is only one major mare, named Moscoviense, on the far side, but there are many on the near side. Scientists hypothesize that just as the Moon's gravitational force causes tides on Earth, Earth's gravitational force probably has an effect on the Moon—especially the side facing Earth. Since there is no proof of water on the Moon, gravity must pull at the crust. The crust likely ruptures and rising lava forms the plains we call mares.

The Far Side

Until 1959, when the then Soviet Union sent the satellite *Lunik 3* all the way around the Moon, we could only guess at what the far side was like. Scientists wrongly assumed that it was the same as the near side. One nineteenth-century astronomer, however, thought that all the Moon's air and water had collected on the far side—along with the Moon's inhabitants!

How strong is the pull of the Moon's gravity?

Being smaller than Earth, the Moon does not have nearly as much gravity. It is enough to cause tides on Earth, but it still is only about 17 percent of Earth's gravity. Say you weighed 100 pounds (45.4 kg) on Earth. If you went to the Moon for summer vacation, you would weigh only 17 pounds (7.7 kg), not counting all the gear you would have to wear to survive. Your walk would be springy, carrying you a few feet with every step.

Does the Moon have an atmosphere?

The Moon's gravity is not strong enough to hold an atmosphere in place. Consequently, the environment above the surface of the planet is uniformly the same as in Earth's exosphere.

THE INNER PLANETS: MERCURY, VENUS, AND MARS

Which are the inner planets?

Mercury, Venus, Earth, and Mars—the first four planets in order from the Sun to the asteroid belt—are called the **inner planets** or terrestrial planets. The inner planets all have hard, solid surfaces (terra means "earth" in Latin). They share other characteristics of Earth that partially result from their proximity to the sun.

What characteristics are shared by the inner planets?

In comparison to the outer planets, the four planets nearest the Sun are remarkably similar: They are all basically made of rock; they are all relatively small; and they are all situated fairly close together. Their surfaces temperatures are relatively hot, ranging from an average of 427°C (806°F) to –23°C (–9°F). Their orbits are relatively quick—they take between 88 days and 687 days to revolve around the Sun.

What is Mercury like?

Mercury is the second smallest planet in the solar system and the planet closest to the Sun. The heat from the Sun is so great on the surface of Mercury that there is no chance of life existing there. It is barren.

Because of its proximity to the bright Sun and its very small size, Mercury is difficult to locate in the sky. It is, however, one of the five planets first identified centuries ago. Mercury seems very similar to the Moon. From Earth, it seems to go through phases, like the Moon; and its crater-filled surface also resembles the Moon.

How can we look at Mercury?

Consider where Mercury is located: an average of 36 million miles from the Sun. Since Mercury never travels far from the Sun, it is not visible at night. But looking for it during the day is dangerous, because of its proximity to the Sun. If you scan the sky—with binoculars, a telescope, or your naked eye—you are likely to locate the Sun before you find Mercury. This will probably cause serious eye damage or loss of sight.

With special sun filters on their telescopes, astronomers study Mercury during the day. For the rest of us, the best time of day to locate this small planet is right after sunset and right before sunrise, when the Sun is still below the horizon. Also, a few times each year, Mercury is at its greatest **elongation**—its greatest distance east or west of the Sun. (For instance, Mercury is farthest east on November 28, 1997, and June 9, 2000; it is farthest west on January 6, 1998, and August 14, 1999.) Within a few days of an elongation, Mercury is easier for astronomers to find.

What does Mercury's orbit look like from Earth?

Mercury orbits the Sun once every 88 days at a speed of 29.8 miles (48 km) per second. Its aphelion (farthest point from the Sun) is at a distance of 43 million miles (69 million km). Mercury's perihelion (closest distance from the Sun) is 30 million miles (46 million km). Because this orbit is not very large, the small planet seems simply to move back and forth in a line from one side of the Sun to the other.

Why are there so many craters on Mercury?

Mercury seems to have been hit by a lot of asteroids. Just under 50 percent of Mercury's

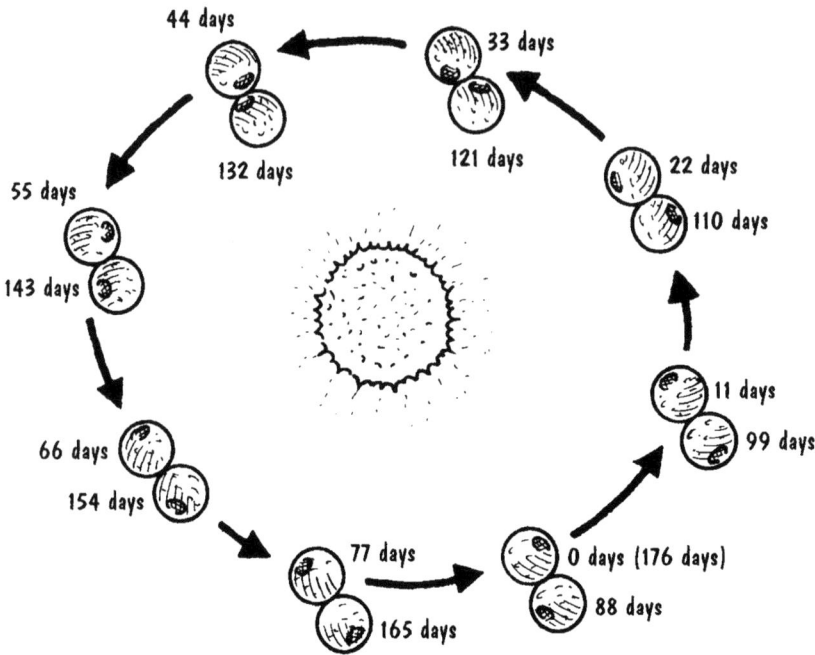

Keep your eye on the small circle, which represents a fixed spot on Mercury's surface. You will see that it takes 176 days for a solar day (from one high noon to the next) to pass.

surface has been photographed by spacecraft. The photos show an average of one hundred to one thousand 6-mile (10-km) craters per each 600,000 square miles (1 million square kilometers).

The appearance of so many craters, their varied sizes, and the fact that they overlap each other (particularly small, or newer, ones over large, or older, ones) tell us that there is little, or little recent, surface erosion on Mercury. A large section of rolling terrain and the presence of mountains, however, suggest that early volcanic activity may have shaped some of the planet.

What is the largest crater on Mercury?

The largest crater photographed so far has been named Beethoven, after the famous composer Ludwig van Beethoven. (Mercury's topographic features are named for famous people, such as Shakespeare and Michelangelo;

exploration ships, including the *Santa Maria*; radar instal-
lations, such as the Russian [Soviet] Vostok; and other
gods, such as the Scandinavian king of gods, Odin.) The
crater Beethoven is 375 miles (625 km) in diameter.

What is the most obvious physical feature on Mercury?

The largest topographic feature seen on Mercury is
the Carolis Basin, a depression as wide as Texas (about
800 miles [1,280 km] in diameter). It is bordered on one
side by tall mountains, called scarps, which can reach
over 1 mile (1.6 km) in height.

What is Mercury made of?

Mercury is thought to be the densest of all the planets, which makes sense when you consider the theory that

Terra Formation

We look at the way land (*terra* in Latin) was formed on
Earth to understand how the surfaces of other terrestrial planets
evolved.

Volcanoes created most of Earth's terrain. Molten material
from Earth's mantle bubbled up 4 billion years ago to form the first
continents. On Mercury, land ridges provide evidence of extreme
volcanic activity in the past. Olympus Mons—the largest known
mountain in the solar system—is one of many extinct volcanoes on
Mars. (Whether there are any active volcanoes left is a matter of
debate.) Between 1990 and 1992, the space probe *Magellan* received
radar signals from Venus's surface that indicated it was largely formed
by volcanic activity. Signs of former lava flows, volcanic explosions, and
hot gases spewing from underground were detected.

Earthquakes, which contribute to the shaping of landscapes, occur
primarily because Earth's terrain rests on shifting plates, called tec-
tonic plates. The shifts create tension in underground rock, which is
released through quakes. Today, earthquakes are believed to be
unique to Earth, though Mars probably experienced them long ago.
Volcanoes can also set off tremors, which probably happened on
Mercury, Venus, and Mars.

Craters are found on all terrestrial planets (for example, Meteor
Crater near Winslow, Arizona). They resulted from collisions with asteroids.

during the early phases of the solar system's formation, the lightest materials were sent farthest into space. For a planet so small to be so dense, it may be mostly solid metal. Scientists believe that Mercury's core, which is 2,100 miles (3,500 km) in diameter, makes up 60 percent of its mass. Because the planet also has a magnetic field, at least some of its metal must be liquid. Rocky silicate material makes up both the crust and mantle (the mantle is a denser form of the crust), which together are about 400 miles (700 km) in depth.

What are the phases of Mercury?

An inferior planet—closer to the Sun—will appear in phases, like the Moon. As Mercury orbits, we generally only see it as a waxing or waning crescent. At a superior conjunction (lined up Earth-Sun-planet), Mercury is full, but it usually can't be seen from Earth because it's behind the Sun. We also cannot see it at inferior conjunction (lined up Earth-planet-Sun), because it gets lost in the light of the Sun. Even if we could see it, it would look like a new moon, almost invisible. Sometimes Mercury transits the Sun and is visible as a speck on the Sun's surface.

Is there an atmosphere on Mercury?

The hydrogen and helium that make up Mercury's very slight atmosphere don't actually originate on the planet. The gases are part of the passing solar wind. The wind is merely slowed by Mercury's gravity before traveling farther into the solar system.

Is a day longer than a year on Mercury?

A Mercurial year (the time it takes for Mercury to revolve around the Sun once) is the equivalent of 88 Earth days (2,112 hours). A Mercurial solar day (the time it takes for the Sun to go from high noon to high noon as seen from Mercury's surface) takes 176 Earth days (4,224 hours)—twice as long as a Mercurial year. After one orbit, Mercury has rotated 1.5 times.

How do astronomers know so many details about Mercury?

Just looking at this small planet doesn't give astronomers much information. Fortunately, electromagnetic waves (mostly radio waves) from Mercury are picked up around the world. They have helped establish the topography and composition of Mercury. Also, twice in 1974 and once in 1975, the spacecraft *Mariner* flew by Mercury and photographed as much of the planet as it could (about 50 percent). Some say that the *Mariner* flight was the most successful information-gathering flight ever made.

What is the planet Venus known for?

Venus, the second planet from the Sun, is sometimes called the twin of Earth; however, there are at least as many differences as similarities. Venus has about the same size, mass, and density as Earth; it is only 24 million miles (40 million km) away from Earth at its closest point; and its orbit is almost as fast as Earth's. It is also hundreds of degrees hotter, completely dry, constantly covered by clouds (yet it is brighter than any star in Earth's sky, except the Sun), and has a crushing atmospheric pressure. Because of Venus's cloud cover, we have never seen its surface from Earth (spacecraft and radio telescopes, however, have taken many radar images of the surface). Perhaps one of the oddest things about Venus is that it rotates backward.

Why does Venus rotate "backward"?

All of the other planets besides Venus (and Pluto) rotate on their axes from west to east, causing the Sun to rise in the east and set in the west. Venus's rotation is called retrograde, moving from east to west. If you could see the Sun rise and set on Venus (which you couldn't because of the cloud cover), the Sun would rise in the west and set in the east. Astronomers don't know specifically why this is so. The most likely explanation is that toward the end of its formation as a planet, a large asteroid slammed into Venus, causing it to reverse its rotation. Such an impact would have come close to shattering the planet.

Is Venus easy to find in the sky?

Like Mercury, Venus is relatively close to the Sun. It is often called the evening or morning star because it is so bright at sunset and sunrise. Venus is the brightest planet in the sky—even brighter than the stars; therefore, it is a pretty easy object to find. As a matter of fact, its brightness is so startling, it is often mistaken for an unidentified flying object (UFO).

Why does Venus shine so brightly?

Oddly enough, Venus is so brilliant because it is covered in clouds. These clouds are about 10 miles (16.5 km) thick and begin about 50 miles (83 km) above the ground. From the surface of a planet, clouds obscure sunlight. From up above, however, they reflect sunlight very brightly. You may notice this if you are in an airplane above Earth's cloud cover. Venus reflects 80 percent of the sunlight it receives.

Why is Venus covered in clouds?

On Earth, clouds are created through water evaporation and condensation. The clouds are water-based. Venus's clouds are made by a process called photochemistry, whereby the Sun's ultraviolet rays react with chemicals in Venus's atmosphere. The clouds around Venus have an acid base—sulfur dioxide.

On Earth, sulfur dioxide is released during volcanic activity. (It's what makes that nasty rotten egg smell in some well water, thermal springs, and volcanic fumes.) The presence of sulfur dioxide clouds supports the argument that active volcanoes exist on Venus.

Venus is permanently covered by clouds.

Do the clouds on Venus move?

They move, but not like clouds on Earth. Venus's atmosphere is very thick and heavy. There are no major temperature or air pressure changes to cause air currents, as on Earth, but Venus's atmosphere rotates around the planet at a fairly steady rate of 225 miles (360 km) per hour. The cloud cover, however, has never broken once in the history of Venusian studies.

Through telescopes fitted with ultraviolet filters, astronomers can make out certain dark patterns on the clouds. By watching the dark spots, they have been able to clock the rotational speed of the clouds. It takes 4 Earth days for Venus's clouds to make one rotation around the planet.

What is Venus's atmosphere made of?

The atmosphere around the second planet from the Sun consists primarily of carbon dioxide (96.5 precent). Nitrogen makes up 3.5 percent of the atmosphere. Traces of gases such as sulfur dioxide, carbon monoxide, hydrochloric acid, and oxygen (0.00003 percent) have also been detected.

What effect does the atmosphere have on Venus?

The two major results of Venus's atmosphere are the amount of pressure it exerts on the planet's surface and the heat it entraps. Carbon dioxide is a heavier gas than nitrogen. Because the atmosphere is more than 96 percent carbon dioxide, the pressure is ninety times greater on Venus than on Earth. Without state-of-the-art, space-age protection, anything landing on Venus from Earth would be instantly crushed. This extreme pressure also traps the planet's natural heat so that it does not dissipate into space.

Venusian Names

On Venus, all topographical features except one are named for women (Venus being a goddess of womanhood). For instance, the main craters include Anna Pavlova (1881–1931), the prima ballerina of her lifetime; Sacajewea (c. 1789–1812?), the Shoshone tribeswoman who explored the West with Lewis and Clark; and Sappho (fl. 610–580 B.C.), the greatest female poet in ancient Greece. Some regions carry other names for Venus: the Greek Aphrodite, the Syrian and Palestinian Ishtar, and Venus in her role as creator, Thetis.

The only feature not named for a woman is the Maxwell mountain range, after the Scottish mathematician James Clerk Maxwell. Why? The mountains were named before it was decided to use only women's names.

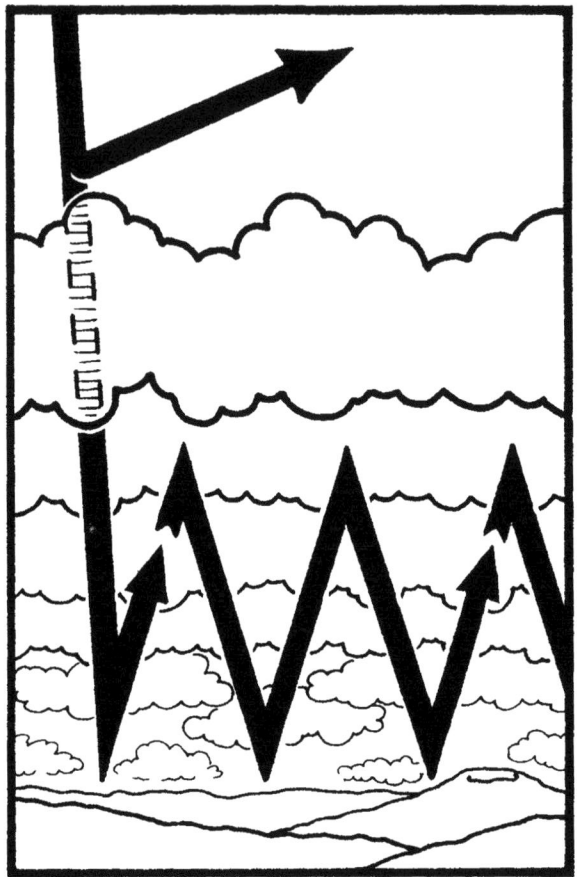

Venus is the brightest and hottest planet in the solar system because it is covered with clouds. The clouds reflect 80 percent of the light from the Sun. While they allow the Sun's ultraviolet rays to pass through, they block the rays' heat from escaping back into space.

How hot is Venus?

Venus is very hot. The surface temperature averages almost 900°F (480°C) around the whole planet. This extreme heat results from the greenhouse effect, which occurs when infrared (heat-producing) rays from the Sun enter an atmosphere and cannot get back out. Carbon dioxide, which makes up 96.5 percent of Venus's atmosphere, lets infrared rays in, but does not release them. It absorbs the rays and radiates their heat. The heat cannot escape into space through Venus's crushing atmospheric pressure. Thus, Venus has earned the title of the hottest planet in the solar system.

What is Venus's surface like?

The first few things you would notice if you could stand on Venus would probably be the heat, the relatively constant calm weather, and the orange-colored rocks and dry dirt at your feet. In general, it might feel like you were in one of the Great Plains states in the middle of a billion-year-long drought. If you looked around, you might see mountains, lava volcanoes, a few craters, and highlands in the distance, but your general impression would probably be that the landscape was pretty flat. There are only 9 miles (15 km) between the lowest and highest points of the planet's surface.

Why aren't there a lot of craters on Venus?

If all those planetesimals and asteroids were flying around some 4 billion years ago—colliding, accreting, and taking chunks out of planets—why don't we see much evidence of them on Venus? Asteroids probably did hit Venus as much as any other planet; they just didn't leave behind much visible evidence. Venus's atmosphere would have burned up any small asteroids. The large bodies that made it through would hit at a relatively slow speed of 12 miles (20 km) per second. The surface would splatter as ejecta, instantly heated to a liquid, or molten, state. Since Venus's surface temperature is so hot, the ejecta would remain liquid and simply flow away.

Does Venus have phases like Mercury?

Because both Venus and Mercury are inferior planets, lying between Earth and the Sun, they exhibit phases—just like the Moon does—as they orbit the Sun. Venus is full during superior conjunction (on the other side of the Sun from Earth) and new during inferior conjunction (between the Sun and Earth). As it cycles from full to new, it appears as a crescent growing thinner with each passing night. From new to full, the planet's crescent waxes, or grows wider, and Venus appears brighter.

Does Venus transit the Sun?

Venus transits the Sun, but not with every revolution. The reason for this is that its orbital plane is at a 3 percent incline to the ecliptic, the Sun's apparent path around Earth. Only when Venus crosses the ecliptic at the time of its inferior conjunction will it transit the Sun. It usually passes above or below the Sun from Earth's point of view. When it does cross the Sun's surface, it appears as a small shadow. This is expected to happen in 2004 and 2012.

How long are Venusian days and years?

The planet makes one rotation on its axis in 243 Earth days. Its solar day—the time it takes the Sun to reappear in the same place in the sky—is 118 Earth days. (On Earth, the two are almost identical, 24 hours, so the Sun rises at approximately the same place every morning. If you lived on Venus, the Sun would rise in quite a different spot along the *western* horizon every morning.)

Venus's days are longer than its years. Venus takes just under 225 Earth days to orbit the Sun; therefore, its year is almost two of the planet's solar days.

How do we know so much about Venus?

A number of unmanned spacecraft have flown by and even landed on the planet to take photographs. The views aren't terribly appealing—dry broken rocks, small mounds, flat terrain—but they are informative. The probes that did land survived a few hours before the conditions on Venus destroyed them. Spacecraft carrying radar have given us the greatest insight into this hot, cloudy world. Over 98 percent of the planet has been mapped.

What is Mars like?

Mars, the closest superior planet to Earth, and the fourth planet from the Sun, frequently looks red, so it is sometimes called the red planet. We know a lot about Mars because it comes closer to Earth than any other planet in favorable opposition (in the best position for viewing) and because we have sent more successful space probes to Mars than to any other planet. Craters, polar ice caps, volcanoes, canyons, plains, and channels show up on the planet's surface. Mars has two distinct seasons: summer and winter. Until the middle of the twentieth century, many people—including astronomers and scientists—thought there was a good chance there was life on Mars.

Is the orbit of Mars circular?

No planet has a truly circular orbit around the Sun. Mars's orbit is particularly elongated, which affects the planet's seasons. Mars takes 788 Earth days to orbit the Sun. At its farthest (aphelion), it is about 155 million miles (250 million km) from the Sun. At its closest (perihelion), Mars is some 130 million miles (210 million km) from the Sun. Mars's orbit approximates a circle that has been elongated by 20 percent; Earth's orbit is only stretched 3 percent away from being a true circle.

What causes seasons on Mars?

Mars's axis is tilted 25.2°, compared to Earth's 23.5°, and Mars is tilted in the same direction. This causes Mars to have summer and winter, like Earth. Martian seasons are longer because it takes Mars longer to orbit the Sun. The seasonal temperatures on Mars stay much colder than on Earth because Mars is farther away from the Sun. The great difference in Mars's aphelion and perihelion cause seasons in the southern hemisphere to be much more extreme than seasons in the northern hemisphere.

What is summer's effect on Mars?

Summer in the southern hemisphere causes the most weather activity on Mars. The temperature increase shrinks the southern polar ice cap (at the same time, the northern ice cap—experiencing winter—grows larger), which increases the air pressure. Increased air pressure causes severe winds to blow toward the equator. The winds can reach up to 90 miles (150 km) per hour, which

New meteoric evidence of possible current or past life on Mars spurred the launch of the Mars Global Surveyor on November 7, 1996. Its mission is to map Mars, study the climate, and further explore the planet's likelihood of supporting rudimentary life.

results in widespread—even planet-wide—dust storms that last up to 6 months.

What is winter like on Mars?

During winter in the southern hemisphere, the polar ice cap grows to cover almost one-quarter of the planet. At the same time, during summer in the northern hemisphere, the northern ice cap is shrinking. Temperatures can reach as low as −190°F (−123°C). Sometimes a frost consisting of water and dust covers the surface. While there are thin clouds in Mars's atmosphere, there is not enough water vapor for precipitation.

What is the temperature on Mars?

Mars is a cold planet. The average air temperature is −22°F (−30°C) in the day and −148°F (−100°C) at night. The highest temperatures occur during the summer at the equator, but even then they hover around freezing.

What are Mars's ice caps made of?

The northern ice cap is permanently frozen water covered by frozen carbon dioxide (dry ice), which solidifies from the atmosphere at cold temperatures. During summer in the north, the ice cap shrinks, as some of the carbon dioxide reverts to gas in the atmosphere. In the winter, it grows much larger again.

The ice cap in the southern hemisphere is almost all frozen carbon dioxide. It also grows and shrinks seasonally, but to a greater extent than the northern cap, as the carbon dioxide solidifies and then vaporizes.

Is there water on Mars?

Evidence of water has fed scientific debates on the possibility of life on Mars for centuries. A well-known twentieth-century astronomer, Percival Lowell, spent his career mapping what he believed were irrigation canals built by Martians. His findings have been proven false, but there are dry channels on Mars that look like they were created by water erosion. There is also evidence of ancient flooding. While water does not now exist on Mars in its liquid form, it does appear as a solid and as vapor.

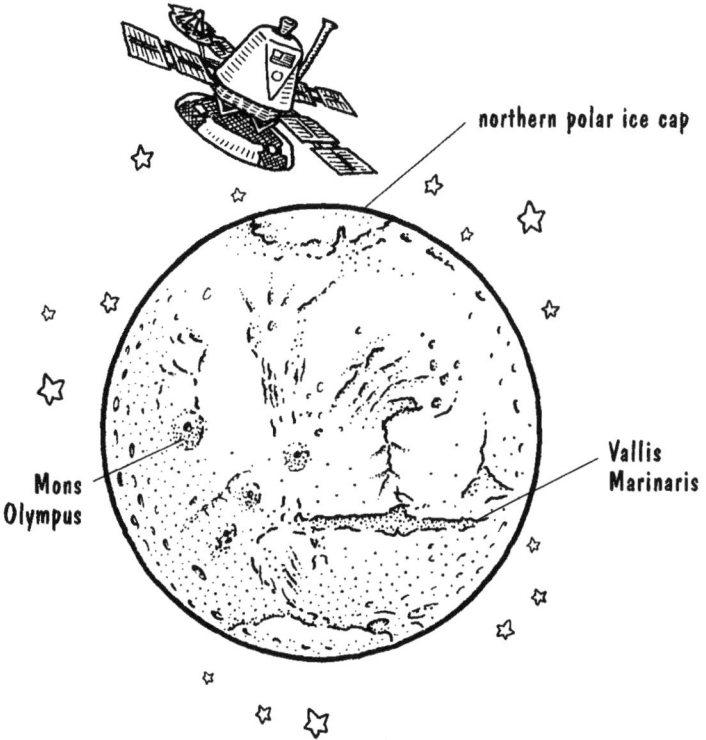

northern polar ice cap

Vallis
Marinaris

Mons
Olympus

Shown here, the most prominent features on Mars are the northern
polar ice cap; the planet's largest volcano, Mons Olympus; lines that
astronomer Percival Lowell mistook for canals; and the Vallis Marinaris,
the largest canyon system.

The northern ice cap is partially ice and sometimes frost,
fog, and water vapor clouds appear.

Is the southern hemisphere older than the northern hemisphere?

More craters are found in the southern hemisphere on
Mars. This makes astronomers think that the surface there
is older than in the northern hemisphere. Something happened in the north—perhaps volcanic activity or water
erosion—to cause craters to disappear.

There is further evidence supporting the astronomers'
theory: the surface of the northern hemisphere is on average 2.5 miles (4 km) lower than that of the south. Another

odd feature of Mars's terrain is a vast area called the Tharsis Bulge near the equator, which sits 6 miles (10 km) higher than the region around it. We don't know why.

What is the highest point on Mars?

Mars is home to the tallest and largest known volcano in the solar system: Mons Olympus. This extinct shield volcano has a base of about 420 miles (700 km) and reaches 15 miles (25 km) into the atmosphere. Its caldera (large opening) measures 53 miles (85 km) in diameter.

By comparison, Mt. Everest, the tallest mountain on Earth, is only 5.5 miles (9 km) high. The largest volcano on Earth is Mauna Kea, which extends 6 miles (10 km) up from the ocean floor.

Mons Olympus is three times as tall as Earth's Mt. Everest. Earth's crust would be unable to support the weight of Mons Olympus.

What is the lowest point on Mars?

Mars has the deepest canyon in the solar system—the Vallis Marinaris, measuring 4.2 miles (6.7 km) deep, 300 miles (500 km) wide, and 2,800 miles (4,500 km) long. The nearby canyons average about 1.8 miles (3 km) deep. The deepest crater on Mars is the Hellas Planitia, some 3.6 miles (6 km) deep.

Mars's Vallis Marinaris measures 4.2 miles (6.7 km) deep; Arizona's Grand Canyon is only 1 mile (1.6 km) deep.

Is there still volcanic activity on Mars?

Mons Olympus, the tallest known volcano—and mountain—in the solar system, is one of many large volcanoes on Mars. It is considered extinct, but some volcanoes may still be active. We have no proof one way or the other.

What is Mars made of?

The planet seems to have a rocky crust approximately 30 miles (50 km) deep. Its mantle is rich in the element silica, like Earth, but it is solid, unlike Earth's partially molten mantle. There is no magnetic field on Mars, so presumably its core is solid. It is likely to be solid iron. While Mars is roughly half the size of Earth, its mass is only about 0.10 percent of Earth's. This leads astronomers to the conclusion that Mars's core is proportionately smaller to the planet than Earth's core is to Earth.

What is Mars's atmosphere like?

Mars's atmosphere is relatively weak. It is so thin that damaging ultraviolet solar radiation makes its way unimpeded to the planet's surface. Carbon dioxide makes up 95 percent of the atmosphere, followed by nitrogen (2.7 percent) and argon (1.6 percent). Oxygen, water vapor, neon, krypton, xenon, and ozone comprise less than 1 percent of the atmosphere on Mars. All of these gases are found in Earth's atmosphere, but in very different percentages. The air pressure on Mars resembles what we expect in a vacuum—almost nil.

Dust clouds exist up to about 12 miles (20 km) above Mars's surface. Clouds of ice crystals (water) lie above the dust. About 18 miles (30 km) up, there is a layer of hazy dust. Carbon dioxide ice clouds are found 30 miles (50 km) from the planet's surface.

Why does Mars appear red?

The surface of Mars is covered in a fine dust that is rich in iron oxide (rust). There are massive winds on the planet that create dust storms, and so a red-pink smog always hangs over it. Consequently, Mars's general appearance is red, but powerful telescopes reveal that the surface is multicolored. Sixty percent of the planet appears red, mostly in the southern hemisphere. The polar ice caps are white and the hard surface under the red dust appears brown or gray and changes to blue-gray during the Martian summer.

Is there life on Mars?

Experiments on Earth have concluded that certain cells can survive a simulated Martian environment. In 1996, a meteorite that originated on Mars was discovered. The announcement that this rock contained possible evidence of life on Mars—or evidence that life once existed on Mars—has sped up plans to send missions back there.

Remember, however, that life existed on Earth for 3 or 4 billion years—and developed under what were likely unique conditions—before it evolved into humankind. Single cell structures, like bacteria, may be the most that

Life on Mars! Big Deal

One of the most intriguing—and fanciful—photographs taken of Mars by *Voyager 1* showed what appeared to be a masklike face of a human being buried just under the surface. Imagine the uproar in the scientific and science fiction communities! The "face on Mars" turned out to be a purely natural surface formation that, when looked at from other angles, was obviously just a clump of rock and dust.

In 1996, a rock sample from Mars was heralded as bearing signs of life. While this discovery made great newspaper headlines, it was not news to scientists. They have known for a long time that evidence for potential life existed "off world." Not only does the universe share all the same building blocks of life, we've already seen evidence of it fall from the sky. Remember that the Murchison meteorite, which fell to Earth in 1969, contained amino acids, nucleic acids, and cellular chemical compounds—all ingredients of life.

can be expected on Mars. Betting on any hominid Martian life-forms is simply a bad bet.

Our fascination with the possibility of humanlike life on Mars stems from the work of one man: Percival Lowell. Lowell lived from 1855 to 1916, and spent much of his life mapping what he called canals on Mars's surface. He claimed that these were manufactured irrigation canals that pointed to the presence of an agricultural civilization on Mars. His detailed maps were a result of seeing what he wanted to see. Canals do not exist on Mars. There are channels—first noted by Giovanni Schiaparelli in 1877 and mistranslated by Lowell as "canals"—dry, winding gorges that probably once were rivers. As Lowell proved, if we aren't careful, we might miss what is on Mars by looking so hard for what we want to find there.

THE OUTER PLANETS: JUPITER, SATURN, URANUS, NEPTUNE, AND PLUTO

What are the outer planets?

The planets that orbit the Sun beyond the asteroid belt are known as the **outer planets**. Besides their location, they share many other similarities—except for Pluto, which is a highly unusual planet. Jupiter, Saturn, Uranus, and Neptune are all much larger than Earth and are made mostly of gas. This has earned them the nickname of gas giants. The outer planets—except for Pluto—are also known as Jovian planets because they resemble the planet Jupiter (*Jove* is the Greek name for "Jupiter").

What characteristics are shared by the outer planets?

Size and composition are the two major characteristics shared by Jupiter, Saturn, Uranus, and Neptune. The smallest outer planet (with the exception of Pluto, which is in a category by itself) is Neptune, and Neptune is almost four times larger than Earth. The outer planets have small cores and huge gaseous outer surfaces. When the Sun developed into a main sequence star, the lightest elements—gases—that were expelled into space traveled the farthest, and they soon became planets. The heavier elements were incorporated into the inner—or terrestrial—planets. The outer planets also all have many satellites orbiting them, from Neptune's eight moons to more than twenty orbiting Saturn.

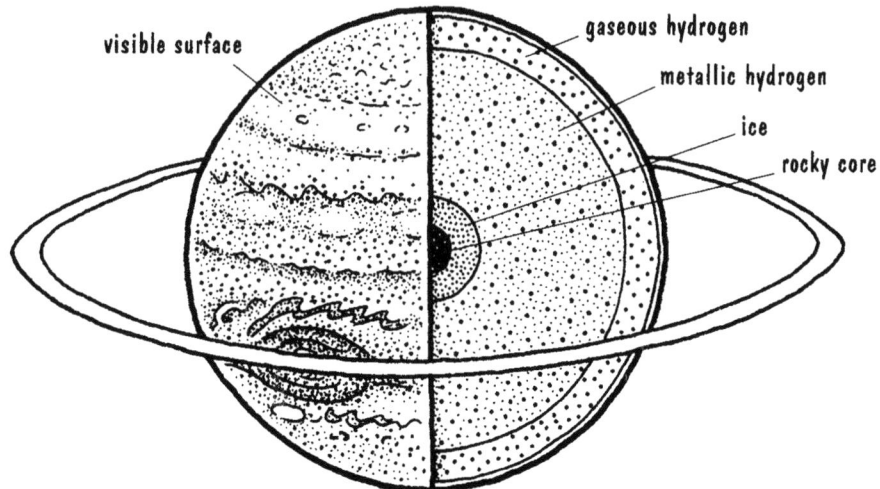

The gas giants—Jupiter, Saturn, Uranus, and Neptune—have small, rocky cores, semisolid mantles, and large outer layers of gases. While Saturn is best known as the ringed planet, all gas giants have ring systems.

What is Jupiter like?

Jupiter is big. It's larger than all the other planets and their moons combined—almost big enough to be a star. Most of its bulk comes from multicolored layers of gases surrounding a relatively small core. The core, however, provides Jupiter with more heat than it gets from the Sun.

When we look at Jupiter, we see the top of a massive orange, brown, and yellow cloud system covering the planet. Fortunately, some of the top clouds are patchy, which gives us a view of the varied belts and zones of gases beneath. This gas giant also emits a lot of electromagnetic radiation, providing astronomers with information about the planet's makeup and activity. Jupiter resembles a solar system all its own, for at least sixteen satellites orbit the planet. Jupiter is also known as the planet with the Great Red Spot.

How big is Jupiter?

If Jupiter had just eighty times more mass, it could be a star; however, if it were a star, Earth would not exist. Jupiter and the Sun would be a binary star system and the solar system would be completely different.

The largest planet in the solar system, Jupiter measures near 88,700 miles (141,920 km) around its equator. The diameter measured from pole to pole, however, is almost 6,000 miles (9,600 km) shorter. This difference in diameter results from Jupiter's fast rotation speed, which causes the equator to bulge, and the poles to flatten out.

What is Jupiter made of?

According to current speculation, Jupiter probably has a small, solid core of silica. Above that lies a thin shell of a different form of liquid hydrogen. Above the liquid lies 600 miles (960 km) of mostly hydrogen and helium gas, with some methane, ammonia, and other gases. The size of Jupiter ensures enough gravity to keep the gases in orbit.

How fast does Jupiter rotate?

Jupiter does not rotate as a solid body does, all at the same speed. Around the equator, the gas layer of Jupiter has a rotation period of 5 hours, 50 minutes, and 30 seconds. Most of the rest of the planet takes 5 minutes and 11 seconds longer to rotate. Various individual sections rotate at still different speeds, and some areas also seem to float back and forth while rotating.

Jupiter's axis is almost vertical. It tilts only 3°; in comparison, Earth's axis has a 23.5° tilt.

What are the different bands that appear across Jupiter?

Some eighteen zones and belts can be identified by their different colors, brightness, spots, and rotation periods. (Zones are dark bands; belts are bright bands.) The main two are the North Equatorial Belt (approximately 7° to 20° latitude) and the South Equatorial Belt (approximately -7° to -21° latitude). Both change in width, with the southern belt being the more variable one.

What causes Jupiter's different colors?

Jupiter's primary gases—hydrogen and helium—are colorless. Trace chemicals within the planet's gas layers, such as methane, ammonia, and phosphine, are responsible for the colors of the belts and zones. The colors range from cream and yellow through pink, orange, and brown to brick red. Brighter areas suggest hotter temperatures; darker areas, cooler ones.

How hot is Jupiter?

Although Jupiter is a great distance from the Sun, it is a relatively hot planet. Scientists have discovered that almost twice as much heat radiates from the planet's rocky core than is received from the Sun. The core's exact temperature is unknown, but it is probably around 30,000°K (53,500°F/30,000°C). Jupiter continues (from the time of its creation) to contract at a rate of about 0.04 inch (1 mm) a year, enough to create great heat. The planet's intense magnetic field (between 1.5 and 7 times greater than Earth's) extends some 4 million miles (6.4 million km) toward the Sun and 400 million miles (640 million km) toward Saturn. All of these factors, plus Jupiter's rapid rotation, add to the planet's overall temperature. These factors also contribute to the variations in temperature throughout Jupiter's complex atmospheric weather system, causing brighter and darker areas within the clouds.

What is the Great Red Spot?

Since the seventeenth century, observers have seen a huge, oval red spot south of Jupiter's equator. The Great Red Spot has a greater surface area than Earth: 8,400 miles (13,440 km) wide by 24,000 miles (38,400 km) long. Scientists have determined that the spot is a huge atmospheric storm. It appears as a hollow, or depression, in Jupiter's cloud cover and is reminiscent of a spiraling cyclone viewed from above. The red spot whirls around itself in a counterclockwise movement, taking 9 days at its center and 12 days at its edge to complete one rotation.

Is Jupiter's Great Red Spot always in the same place?

The spot usually can be found 22° south of the equator, in or near the South Equatorial Belt. While it does vary in longitude, and can disappear from view for months or even years, it is almost always at this latitude.

Is the Great Red Spot permanent?

We don't know whether or not the Great Red Spot will disappear for good one day. Storms on Earth sooner or later die out, but the Great Red Spot has reportedly been around for nearly three centuries. Beginning in 1901, Jupiter exhibited a similar, though smaller, spot called the Great Disturbance. Its disappearance in 1940 led scientists to question anew whether the Great Red Spot will also vanish one day. The Great Red Spot has been shrinking since it was first discovered, and is about one-half of its original size; however, its massive size may keep it going, if not forever, as long as we are here to observe it.

How many moons orbit Jupiter?

Jupiter has sixteen known satellites, but astronomers believe there could be more. The discovery of the four largest—Ganymede, Callisto, Io, and Europa—is credited to Galileo, who recorded them in 1610. The average diameter of the Galilean moons measures 2,540 miles (4,230 km), whereas the average diameter of the other Jovian moons is a mere 40 miles (67 km). We can't discern much detail about the smaller moons from Earth.

A celestial object recorded in the fourth century B.C. in China may have been Jupiter's moon Ganymede. This calls into question whether Galileo was really the first to identify Jovian moons.

Do all the moons revolve around Jupiter together?

They all revolve around their host planet, Jupiter, but their orbits are different in distance, speed, and inclination of orbital plane. This all makes for quite a bit of activity. Jupiter's moons act something like a microcosm (miniature version) of the solar system, and astronomers have learned a lot about the whole solar system by studying them.

How far away from Jupiter do the moons orbit?

Jupiter's sixteen known moons travel in three distinct groups. The first, including the four Galilean moons, ranges from 77,000 miles (124,000 km) to over 600,000 miles (960,000 km). The next group orbits from 6.6 million miles (10.56 million km) to almost 7.2 million miles (11.52 million km) away. The third family of satellites is almost twice as far away from the planet as the middle group: around 13 million miles (20.8 million km) to 14 million miles (22.4 million km).

How fast do Jupiter's moons orbit?

Astronomers frequently use orbital period (how long one revolution takes) to measure speed instead of miles (kilometers) per hour. The three families of satellites are clustered by period as well as distance. Of the four closest moons, none takes more than 1 day to orbit Jupiter. The four Galilean moons, also in the nearest family, take between 1.8 and 17 days. The middle satellite group takes about 250 days. The farthest four moons take from 617 to 758 days to complete their orbits. The satellites in the last group also travel in a retrograde direction; that is, in an opposite direction from the others.

What is Ganymede like?

Ganymede, made mostly of ice and rock, is the third farthest Galilean moon from Jupiter and is the planet's largest satellite. Its surface is cratered, like Jupiter's farthest moon, Callisto, and our Moon, but there are large areas of ridges and valleys. This seems to result from tension due to the stretching of Ganymede's surface. Some areas split to form grooves while the surrounding area remains high. Water appears to seep out from under the moon's surface, which causes some of the craters and valleys to appear very bright.

What is Europa like?

This Galilean moon orbits Jupiter between Io and Ganymede. Europa is about the same size as Earth's moon. It has a surface of ice, though ice probably makes up only 10 percent of its composition. The other 90 percent is rock. A system of low ridges covers Europa, making it look like a cracked egg. Its relatively smooth surface is believed to be caused by an ocean of liquid water beneath the thin crust of ice. The ocean remains liquid because Europa's neighbor Ganymede acts like our Moon, causing ocean tides. The motion of the water is sufficient to keep it liquid under the thin ice.

What is Io like?

Rocky Io is the closest Galilean moon to Jupiter. The craters that mark its surface are volcanic craters, not the result of meteorite bombardment. The tallest volcanoes are about 5.5 miles (8.8 km) high. Instead of molten rock, sulfur compounds spew out of Io's volcanoes, covering evidence of any impact craters and giving the moon a new crust—including hot lakes of sulfur—some few tenths of an inch (centimeter) thick every century or so. Spacecraft observations have noted volcanic matter being ejected some 180 miles (300 km) skyward every few seconds. Io's volcanic activity comes from a gravitational tug-of-war between Jupiter on the one side and the moons Europa and Ganymede on the other.

Io orbits Jupiter within the planet's magnetic field, which causes a channel of electricity—like a high-tension wire. The currents exceed 3 million amps, and great auroras result where the channel meets Jupiter's atmosphere.

Jupiter's nearby moon Io has many constantly active volcanoes. Instead of releasing lava, as volcanoes do on Earth, they spew sulfur compounds. Io receives vast amounts of radiation from Jupiter, making it one of the most deadly environments in the solar system.

What is Callisto like?

The farthest Galilean moon from Jupiter, Callisto is mostly made of ice and rock. Its surface shows many craters, but unlike our Moon craters, these are rather shallow with low walls encircling them. Callisto's craters were probably partially filled in by a blanket of ice moving across the moon's surface like a glacier. Some bright spots on this relatively dark satellite indicate new craters, which the ice has not yet deformed.

What is the planet Saturn like?

Saturn is known as the planet with the rings around it, although Jupiter, Uranus, and Neptune also have rings. These rings, which encircle the sixth planet at its equator, have distinct characteristics. The planet itself is a gas giant quite light in density and bright in luminosity. Its surface sometimes reveals a Great White Spot, similar to Jupiter's Great Red Spot. The planet is covered in clouds and is subject to a strong wind system. Eighteen satellites orbit Saturn.

How many rings does Saturn have?

The answer depends on how you count them. Seven of Saturn's ring systems have been identified and named by scientists, but some of those rings are made up of countless thin rings that parallel each other. There could be thousands of them!

The seven major rings are named for the first seven letters of the alphabet. Since the rings were not discovered in linear order, their sequence, beginning closest to Saturn, runs like this: D, C, B, A, F, G, and E. C, B, and A are Saturn's major rings. Between B and A, the two rings most visible from Earth, there is a large space known as the **Cassini division**.

What are Saturn's rings made of?

Astronomers believe that Saturn's rings are made of water, ice, and rock. This icy matter can range from the size of a tiny grain of sand to bigger than a boulder—over 30 feet (9 meters) across. The particles probably came from passing comets or moons that got too close to Saturn and were broken up; the space debris was then caught in the planet's force of gravity. Or perhaps the rings are composed of remnants of the Sun's explosion into adulthood: particles of solar matter that never coalesced into moons or planets.

How large are Saturn's rings?

The whole system of rings—gaps and all—begins about 40,000 miles (64,000 km) out from Saturn's equator and ends 290,000 miles (464,000 km) from the surface. That's 250,000 miles (400,000 km) of rings and gaps. The particles are not spread out on a single plane, but the rings are very thin. Compared to the great distance the rings reach, their width is minute: only a few miles (kilometers) thick. The size of the individual rings varies. The largest ring, the B ring, extends for 15,000 miles (24,000 km).

Rings of Saturn

Name	Distance from Saturn (thousands of miles/km)	Rotational period around Saturn (hrs)	Description
D	40/67	4.91	Not visible from Earth
C	44/73	5.61	The dusky or crepe ring; semitransparent
B	55–70/88–112	7.93–11.41	Most prominent Cassini division eccentric ring(s)
A	73–81/121–135	11.92–14.14	Surrounds Encke division
F	85/141	14.94	Single eccentric ring; discovered by *Pioneer 11*
G	100–104/166–174	18–21	Not visible from Earth; discovered by *Voyager 1*
E	108–288/180–480	4–22	Highly diffuse; not visible from Earth

Do the rings orbit Saturn?

Saturn's rings have circular orbits, but they revolve at various speeds. Parts of a single ring even orbit at different rates. For instance, the outer edge of ring E (furthest from the planet) has an orbital period of 4 hours, but the inner edge (some 180,000 miles [288,000 km] closer) takes 22 hours to orbit. The E ring has both the slowest and fastest orbits of all the rings.

Can we always see Saturn's rings?

Rings D, E, and G are not visible from Earth at all. We only discovered E and G by sending up spacecraft. The system as a whole circles the planet at its equator. Saturn's axis, around which the planet rotates, is tilted 26.7° in relation to its equator, so that sometimes the southern hemisphere is tilted toward the Sun (and Earth), and sometimes the northern hemisphere faces the Sun (and Earth). Sometimes we can see the rings clearly, but at other times, they appear "edge on" and are invisible. (Remember that the rings are only a few miles [kilometers] thick.) On an average of every 14 years and 9 months, the edges of Saturn's rings face us. The next edge-on view will be in 2010.

Which rings are the most prominent?

Ring B is the largest and brightest ring around Saturn. It orbits the planet at a distance of 55,000 to 70,000 miles (88,000 to 112,000 km). The B ring is made up of thousands of smaller concentric rings that are so close to each other, they are indistinguishable from each other when viewed from Earth. B-ring ice particles are light-colored and tightly packed, making the ring seem bright and opaque. The inner edge of the B ring is the brightest point in the ring system.

The second most obvious ring is A. It is separated from the B ring by the Cassini division. Similar in makeup to ring B, ring A simply has fewer particles. It is neither as bright nor as opaque, but it is made of thousands of ringlets. Within the 8,500-mile (13,600-km) band of the A ring lies the **Encke division**.

What divisions are in the ring system?

The two most prominent divisions in Saturn's ring system are the Cassini division and the Encke division, named for their discoverers. The Cassini division extends for 2,100 miles (3,360 km) between rings A and B. The

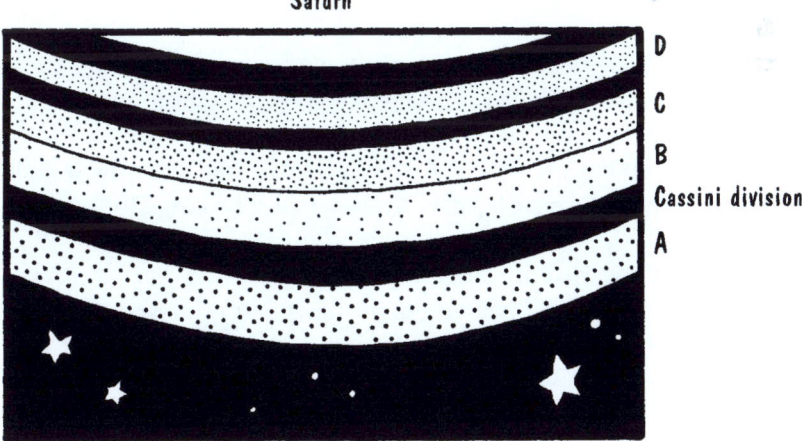

The cause of the Cassini division (the gap between Saturn's B and A rings) is not well understood. One theory is that the syncopation of the ring particles' orbits and the orbit of the moon Mimas causes the particles to settle in ring A or B, but to leave the division clear.

200-mile (320-km) Encke division lies within ring A. These divisions appear to be gaps between rings, allowing us to see through to the planet's surface, but they really have small ringlets of their own. Some of the ringlets within the divisions, however, orbit Saturn eccentrically.

Are there different types of rings?

Idiosyncratic rings around Saturn are rare and, for the most part, inexplicable. They do not conform to the laws of physics as we understand them. The primary rings, A through G, orbit Saturn in circles. According to physics, it should be impossible for a ring to do otherwise—to have an elliptical (oval-shaped) orbit, for example. Eccentric rings, however, have elliptical orbits. The particles in kinky rings do not orbit in a regular pattern, but clump together and spread out irregularly, which shouldn't be possible. Braided rings are ringlets that seem to overlap each other in the pattern of a braid. Again, physics should make this impossible. The likely explanation has to do with the gravity of moons orbiting within the bands of atypical rings, but we really don't understand how this happens.

What is Saturn made of?

Within the rings lies the second largest planet in the solar system: Saturn. Its composition is similar to that of its next door neighbor, Jupiter—mostly hydrogen and helium gases. The planet's ice-covered core of iron and silica is just a little bit bigger than Earth. Compressed hydrogen around the core resembles a metal, and is surrounded by a thick outer layer of hydrogen and helium gases.

How hot is Saturn?

Saturn generates more heat than it receives from the Sun. It has lost the heat caused by its formation, but helium drops "rain" down from the atmosphere—mostly hydrogen—which creates heat. The cloud-top temperature ranges around −300°F (−200°C).

How fast does Saturn rotate?

Because Saturn is made mostly of gas, it has varying rotation speeds. Because Earth is solid, its rotation period

Saturn has severe winds; winds whip around the equator in a jet stream some 50,000 miles (80,000 km) wide at speeds around 1,120 miles (1,800 km) per hour.

is 24 hours at every latitude. Latitudes nearer the poles, however, have a shorter distance to travel in 24 hours, so they rotate more slowly. Since Saturn is not bound together in a solid form, the gases at different latitudes rotate at different speeds and with different rotation periods, depending on their composition. The planet's core rotates once every 10 hours, 39 minutes, and 24 seconds. Around the equator, the gas is faster, taking 10 hours and 14 minutes for one rotation. Near the poles, the rotation period is 10 hours and 40 minutes. Saturn's fast rotation causes an equatorial bulge about 480,000 miles (768,000 km) larger than the polar diameter.

How do we know Saturn's core rotation period?

Saturn has a very strong magnetic field. Spacecraft sent to study the planet recorded regularly pulsing radio waves to determine the core's rotational speed. The magnetic field on Saturn is at least 500 times (some say 1,000 times) stronger than Earth's magnetic field. Saturn's magnetic poles are almost exactly aligned with its geographic north and south poles, though magnetic north is at the south pole and vice versa.

What is Saturn's Great White Spot?

Similar to Jupiter's Great Red Spot, a white spot on Saturn reveals the presence of a huge atmospheric storm. Unlike Jupiter's ever-present spot, Saturn's white spot appears only periodically, approximately every 30 years. First identified in 1876, the spot has appeared more or less on schedule ever since. It is located near the equator and can be seen for several months at a time.

How many satellites orbit Saturn?

Saturn not only has its many rings, it is also endowed with more known moons than any other planet. Some eighteen moons have been named and astronomers suspect—are even sure—that several more exist. The closest named moon to the planet is Pan, a body some 12 miles (19.2 km) in diameter. Pan moves around Saturn about once every 12 hours at a distance of 80,000 miles (128,000

Saturn's density is so slight that if there were an ocean large enough to contain it, it would probably float! While more than 700 Earths would be needed to fill up Saturn's volume, the planet's gravity is just barely more than that of Earth.

km). The farthest moon is Phoebe, at almost 8 million miles (13 million km), and may be a trapped asteroid. It measures 18 × 120 × 125 miles (30 × 200 × 210 km) and makes one revolution in over 1.5 years (550 days). Saturn's largest, and perhaps most interesting, moon is Titan.

What is Titan like?

Saturn's largest and brightest moon, Titan, seems to hold some ingredients for life, such as a nitrogen atmosphere, chemical interaction with sunlight, landmasses, water, silicates, and carbon dioxide. Unfortunately, its nitrogen and methane atmosphere, which hangs like a dense, orange smog, blocked detection of any surface detail by the *Voyager* spacecraft mission (1980). Theoretical models of the surface predict a huge ocean of liquid methane broken up either by rocky land or masses of frozen methane, water, and/or carbon dioxide. Chemical reactions in the atmosphere are similar to those believed to have created a friendly environment for life early in Earth's development. The temperature on Titan, −290°F (−190°C), however, makes life impossible. Perhaps when the Sun becomes a red giant in about 5 billion years, and grows beyond Mars's orbit, Titan's surface will heat up enough to eventually support life. Unfortunately, it is precisely the intensely cold temperature that holds Titan's atmosphere together by slowing down molecular movement. If the atmosphere heated up, its molecules would move fast enough to escape into space. Titan might become warm enough for life, but in doing so it would lose its atmosphere. Without an atmosphere, life on Titan could not survive.

What is the planet Uranus like?

Uranus is the third gas giant and the seventh planet from the Sun. The planet's equator rotates about where we would expect to find the north and south poles. Uranus appears to be a smooth, pale blue orb, but we can't see through the atmosphere to the surface. We aren't even sure where the planet ends and the atmosphere begins! We do know that Uranus, like Saturn, has rings, but they are not as obvious. It's a cold, slow, distant planet with fifteen moons. Uranus is best known for its odd rotational tilt.

When was Uranus discovered?

William Herschel (1738–1822) was a musician who began to study the mathematical foundation of harmony. Mathematics led him to astronomy, and, with the help of his sister, Caroline, Herschel set out to map every star in the northern hemisphere with a magnitude of 4 or greater. Through his detailed and methodical observations, Herschel found and identified Uranus as a planet in 1781.

How is Uranus's rotation tilted?

Uranus's axis is tilted in a peculiar way. Earth's axis tilts at 23.5°; Uranus's axis tilts at 97.9°, which is at more than a right (90°) angle. (Imagine Earth's poles being located near the equator!) The planet, however, still

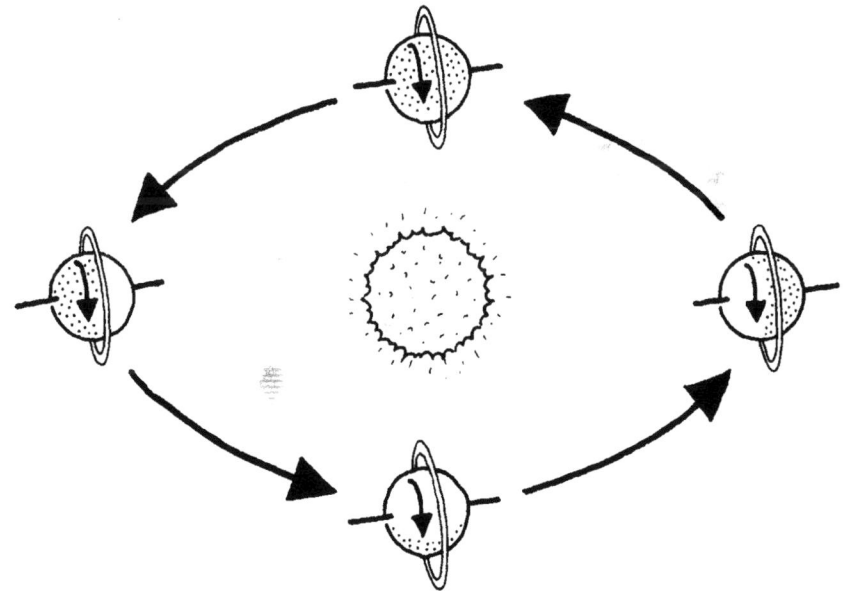

Since Uranus's axis is tilted more than 90° from the vertical plane, the planet appears to rotate on its side. Technically, Uranus has a retrograde rotation—in the opposite direction from most other planets.

The Tilted Planet

To get a sense of Uranus's unique rotation and revolution, you may want to create a model of it. This is easy enough to do. Find a ball, or other spherical object, and mark an equator and a north and south pole on it. Hold the ball with the north pole at the top and begin a typical west-to-east rotation. While continuing the rotation, tilt the ball to the left slightly more than one-quarter of a circle. (You may need to use two hands.) The north pole will end up just below where the ball's equator was. You will see that the rotation has magically become an east-to-west rotation.

As you hold the ball in front of you, imagine that you are the Sun. While keeping the rotation going, aim the north pole toward yourself. Begin moving the ball in orbit around yourself: pole to equator to pole to equator. Notice that the poles receive a lot of sunlight before the equator gets a chance at some. That's their 42-year-long day and 42-year-long night.

rotates around its north-south axis. Because it is tilted more than 90°, Uranus's rotation is technically retrograde: from east to west rather than from west to east, as on Earth. Because Uranus is a gas giant, the planet has varying rotational speeds.

Why is Uranus's axis tilted?

We don't have any physical evidence to answer this question. Judging by what we've seen elsewhere in the solar system, astronomers suppose that, early in Uranus's formation, a huge meteorite or other body knocked it on its side.

How does Uranus's axial tilt effect its orbit?

As Uranus orbits the Sun, first the north pole faces the solar surface, then the equator, then the south pole, and then the equator again. Uranus, a relatively slow planet, takes 84 Earth years to orbit the Sun.

How long is Uranus's day?

A sidereal day equals one planetary rotation. A single rotation takes Uranus 17 hours and 54 minutes. If we think in terms of a solar day—how long it takes the Sun to go from high noon to high noon—we get a different picture. The combined effect of Uranus's tilted rotation and slow orbit causes the planet's poles to experience 42-year-long solar days.

What are the effects of Uranus's cold temperature?

Voyager 2 registered a nearly consistent temperature of −155°F (−221°C) on Uranus. Strong winds—up to 180 miles (288 km) per hour—that blow in the same direction as Uranus rotates keep the temperature steady all around the planet.

The cold is responsible for our inability to see any surface detail on this pale blue planet. The atmosphere is similar to Jupiter's and Saturn's atmospheres: 85 percent hydrogen, 13 percent helium, and 2 percent methane. But the cold temperatures on Uranus create a low, dense smog covering the typically stormy atmosphere and the planet's surface.

What is Uranus's interior like?

Uranus lacks a distinct equatorial bulge and an interior source of heat, which means that it probably does not have a molten or liquid interior. Its core is likely rock, such as the other gas giants have, surrounded by a 6,000-mile-thick (9,600-km-thick) layer of ice made from ammonia, methane, and water. A layer of hydrogen, helium, and methane gases extends to the cloud tops.

What are Uranus's rings like?

The eleven rings around Uranus are thin bands some 0.6 to 7.0 miles (1 to 11 km) thick; the exception is the farthest edge of the farthest ring, which ranges up to 60 miles (96 km). They are made mostly of ices, with very little dust. Generally, rings occur as dust particles collide with each other within an orbit. Astronomers could not figure out what had happened to the dust until *Voyager* studied Uranus's atmosphere. It turns out that the atmosphere extends higher up than expected—up into the rings. The hydrogen in the atmosphere slows down the dust molecules, causing them to fall out of orbit. This means that Uranus's rings are disintegrating and, one day, will disappear.

Discovery of the Planet Herschel?

Sir Frederick William Herschel, born in 1738, led a varied and distinctive life. As a young man, he witnessed the Seven Years' War in Europe while playing oboe in a military band. His music skills, and his winning personality, earned him an organist position in Bath, England. While there, his studies in musical harmony led him to take up mathematics. Mathematics led him to optics. Optics gave way to telescopes and, consequently, astronomy.

Herschel set about improving contemporary telescopes. With the help of his sister, Caroline, born in 1750, he fashioned them in his kitchen. Not a wealthy man, he used horse manure as a mold for the telescopes' mirrors.

William and Caroline set out to map the sky, not a small task. Employed during the day at his organ, William worked nights systematically viewing and recording the stars, planets, and comets. According to Caroline, sleep was not much of a consideration.

In 1781, William noticed a strange star. He thought it was a comet perhaps. A friend of William's told Nevil Maskelyne, King George III's astronomer royal, of his find. Maskelyne was the first to suggest that this peculiar star was a planet. Six months later, the new planet was confirmed by a Swedish astronomer and two French mathematicians.

The discovery of the new planet earned William and Caroline royal pensions. This made Caroline the first woman to become a professional astronomer.

Naming the new planet turned out to be a problem. William ignored the task, while others put forth such names as Herschel, Uranus, Neptune, and Astraea. Finally, William suggested Georgium Sidus, which means George's Star, after his patron. But the planet wasn't a star. For 66 years, the planet was variously known as Herschel, Uranus, and the Georgian Planet. In 1847, an almanac referred to the planet as Uranus, and the name stuck.

William remained a leader in the field of astronomy until his death in 1822. Caroline, who continued to help her brother and discovered some eight comets herself, survived him by 26 years. The Herschel legacy was carried on by William's son John, who surveyed stars in the Southern Hemisphere.

William Herschel never accepted the possibility of luck, or chance, in his discovery of Uranus. As a consummate scientist, he believed it was a case of thorough observation and research: simply, a good job, well done.

How many moons does Uranus have?

Before the space age, we knew of five satellites orbiting Uranus: Miranda, Ariel, Umbriel, Titania, and Oberon. (The names came from the works of Shakespeare and the poet Alexander Pope.) Ten more moons, discovered by *Voyager*, are small, dark bodies of methane ices. Of the fifteen known moons, only Titania and Oberon—the two largest—are visible to the naked eye.

What are Uranus's two largest moons like?

Titania and Oberon—the largest and most distant satellites—show different signs of cratering. On Titania, the craters are small, which probably means that the original large craters were eroded by some kind of geological force. Astronomers believe that large surface cracks—over 600 miles (960 km) long and 3 miles (5 km) deep—exuded slushy ice after large meteors hit the surface. After the period of bombardment, Titania's interior cooled to solid ice, leaving the cracks above visible.

Oberon has no cracks, but it does display a geologic time line of craters—from early, large impacts to later, smaller ones. While the surface seems to have remained mostly unchanged, melted matter from its interior has apparently leaked out to cover the floors of some craters.

Both of these moons are rockier than expected. The ice under their surfaces is probably not pure water, since the moons do not get warm enough to melt water ice. Methane clathrate, a mixture of methane and water, melts at a lower temperature, and is likely the composition of the moons' ice.

What is Miranda like?

Miranda, the closest of Uranus's large moons, has a varied surface of craters, valleys, faults, ridges, and canyons. Three large regions have ridges and valleys reminiscent of a plowed field. One of the regions displays a large V-shape called a chevron. A system of canyons, some as deep as 12 miles (19 km), can be seen on Miranda, as well as ice cliffs soaring 12 miles (20 km) high. Astronomers believe that the varied land formations of this rocky, icy moon may have resulted from a number of severe collisions or the gravitational force of nearby Ariel.

In 2011, Neptune will complete its first orbit since it was discovered in 1846.

What is Neptune like?

Neptune is the smallest of the gas giants, and the farthest from the Sun. Its discovery, in 1846, came about through mathematical calculation, rather than simple observation. We knew little about Neptune before 1989, when the spacecraft *Voyager 2* began photographing it. (*Voyager* could observe only the southern hemisphere, as the northern was covered in darkness.) This relatively small, bright blue planet is simply just too far away for detailed observation from Earth. The *Voyager* photographs revealed some similarities to Neptune's neighboring gas giants: varying rotational speed, strong winds, several distinct dark and light spots on its surface, an internal heat source, rings, and moons.

How was Neptune discovered?

The search for Neptune began when astronomers noticed that Uranus's movements, particularly its orbit, didn't correspond to their expectations. One explanation was that another planet existed beyond Uranus, and exerted its gravitational force on Uranus. In 1846 astronomers calculated exactly where such a planet would have to be, pointed their telescopes to that spot in the sky, and found Neptune!

Why is Neptune's atmosphere bright blue?

Neptune has an atmosphere of hydrogen, helium, and methane, just as Uranus does. The methane, which lies in a haze over the planet's thick cloud cover, absorbs the red end of the spectrum, reflecting the blues.

What are winds like on Neptune?

The winds around Neptune's equator blow at a rate of almost 1,500 feet (450 m) per second, or just over 1,000 miles (1,600 km) per hour, making the smallest gas giant also one of the windiest. The equatorial winds blow in the opposite direction (east to west) from Neptune's rotation. Approximately 50° further south, the winds taper off to

1,000 feet (300 m) per second and change to blow back in the direction of the planet's rotation.

What is Neptune's Great Dark Spot?

Neptune's Great Dark Spot—like Jupiter's Great Red Spot and Saturn's Great White Spot—indicates an atmospheric storm. It is an anticyclone (a cyclone rotating in a counterclockwise direction) about the size of Earth that travels eastward about 8° south of the equator at a pace of 100 feet (30 m) per second. About 42° south, Scooter—a spot with a bright center—rotates much more quickly. Still farther south, at 55°, is another dark spot. Over these spots rise high, white wisps of methane ice crystals similar to Earth's cirrus clouds.

What is Neptune's interior made of?

Neptune has a partly rocky, but mostly icy, core which may not be completely distinct from its mantle, or middle layer. The mantle seems to be made of water, ammonia, and methane in ice form. It is surrounded by gaseous forms of hydrogen, helium, and methane in the atmosphere.

How cold is Neptune?

Neptune is over 1 billion miles (1.6 billion km) farther away from the Sun than Uranus, but the two planets are close in temperature: −365°F (−220°C) on Neptune; −355°F (−214°C) on Uranus. This results from Neptune's interior, which is not as solid as Uranus's. A partially fluid core will experience more movement than a solid core, and movement—friction—creates heat. While Neptune is not hotter than Uranus, it is much warmer than expected, given its distance from the Sun.

What is Neptune's ring system like?

Neptune has at least five discernible rings made of microscopic particles of dust. They are so thin, diffuse, and uneven that all but one disappear at some point. The system begins about 10,000 miles (16,000 km) above Neptune's clouds and extends for 13,000 miles (21,000 km). The widest ring, called the Plateau, stretches for almost 2,500 miles (4,000 km). The thinnest ring is only 18 miles (30 km) wide.

How many moons does Neptune have?

Neptune has eight moons. The two largest—Nereid and Triton—were discovered soon after the planet itself, and the other six were identified by *Voyager 2*. Of all the satellites, Triton has the most interesting detail. It is the only known moon in the solar system that orbits its host in an opposite direction from the planet's rotation. In fact, astronomers have said that Triton's orbit is more like that of a comet than a satellite. Triton is smaller than Earth's moon, only 140 miles (225 km) in diameter, and is the coldest place in the solar system: −393°F (−236°C). Triton, Neptune's second-to-farthest satellite, orbits at a distance of 215,000 miles (345,000 km).

Why is Pluto different from the other outer planets?

Why Pluto is so different is not well understood, but it is obviously a unique planet. It is the farthest planet from the Sun, the smallest planet, and resembles the terrestrial planets more than its Jovian neighbors.

Pluto has a peculiar orbit. It crosses Neptune's orbital path so that at certain times Neptune is actually the farthest planet from the Sun. Coming as it does after the four gas giants, this stony, tiny planet with an irregular orbit holds many questions for astronomers.

What is Pluto like?

We know very little about Pluto because no spacecraft has gone near it, and its small size and great distance make observation difficult. Pluto is 3.6 billion miles (5.8 billion km) from Earth. It would take more than 45 million Earths placed side by side to cover the distance between the two planets. Like Neptune, Pluto was discovered as a result of mathematical computation. Its orbit is decidedly irregular, and Pluto's origins are debated, in the scientific community, but even more so in the media.

How big is Pluto?

Pluto is the smallest planet in the solar system, with a diameter of 1,425 miles (2,280 km)—which is less than half the width of the United States, about 50 percent of the size of Mercury, and 66 percent the size of Earth's moon. Pluto's moon, Charon, has a diameter of about 739 miles (1,182 km).

How was Pluto discovered?

When astronomer William Herschel identified Uranus in 1781, astronomers determined that there must be at least one more planet beyond it to cause the idiosyncracies of its orbit. This led to the discovery of Neptune in 1846. But even Neptune's existence did not justify the peculiarities of Uranus's orbit. Another planet had to exist. Through mathematical computation, scientists pinpointed where this ninth planet—Planet X—should be. In 1930, after 25 years of concerted searching by astronomers, Clyde Tombaugh of the Lowell Observatory, in Arizona, found Pluto.

Is Pluto a planet?

Some astronomers have questioned whether Pluto should be classified as a planet, rather than an errant moon or an asteroid. It does not generate light; it is less massive than a star; it wanders through constellations; and it orbits the Sun—just like the other planets. Pluto's orbit, however, is decidedly peculiar. All planets "wander" through constellations, which shows that they are not fixed in one place like stars are; because of Pluto's orbital inclination, however, it travels through constellations that no other planet visits. Pluto's orbit crosses another planet's path; no other planet does that.

One of the definitions of a planet is that it appears as a disk, not a point of light, in the sky. Not even the most powerful telescopes on Earth were able to show Pluto as a disk until 1985, when Pluto's moon eclipsed the planet. This provided astronomers in Hawaii with the data necessary to map Pluto's surface features. Pluto, while irregular, meets the minimum requirements for a planet, but some believe it is really a planetesimal from the Kuiper Belt, or an escaped moon from Neptune.

Is Pluto Planet X?

When Uranus was discovered in 1781, astronomers concluded that yet another, more distant, planet had to exist. Something, they figured, was exerting a strong gravitational influence on Uranus's orbit. They called that something Planet X. The search for Planet X led to the identification of Neptune, but Neptune was not strong enough alone to so effect Uranus's orbit. Planet X was still out there somewhere.

Many astronomers hoped that the discovery of Pluto would solve the mystery of Planet X and Uranus's orbit. But even Pluto doesn't measure up to astronomer's expectations of Planet X. The major problem is its size. Pluto is about half the size of Mercury and has only 0.2 percent the mass of Earth. According to the laws of physics, it is not big enough to cause the oddities in Uranus's and Neptune's orbits, which led to the idea of Planet X in the first place. Massive searches have been conducted in the region of Pluto, but no other possible Planet X has yet been found. Some astronomers believe the real Planet X is still somewhere out there.

How is Pluto's orbit irregular?

Pluto's perihelion (closest point) is 4.4 billion miles (7 billion km) from the Sun. Its aphelion (farthest point) is 7.4 billion miles (11.8 billion km). This usually makes Pluto the farthest planet from the Sun, but not always. Pluto's orbit crosses the path of Neptune's orbit, and for 20 years out of its almost 250-year orbit, Pluto is closer to the Sun than Neptune. From 1979 to 1999, Neptune is the most distant planet in the solar system.

Why don't Pluto and Neptune collide?

Since the tiny Pluto crosses the gas giant's path, it is reasonable to think that the two would collide. Perhaps Pluto would get caught by the larger planet's gravitational force and become a satellite. This doesn't happen because Pluto's orbital inclination (the angle of its orbital plane) is

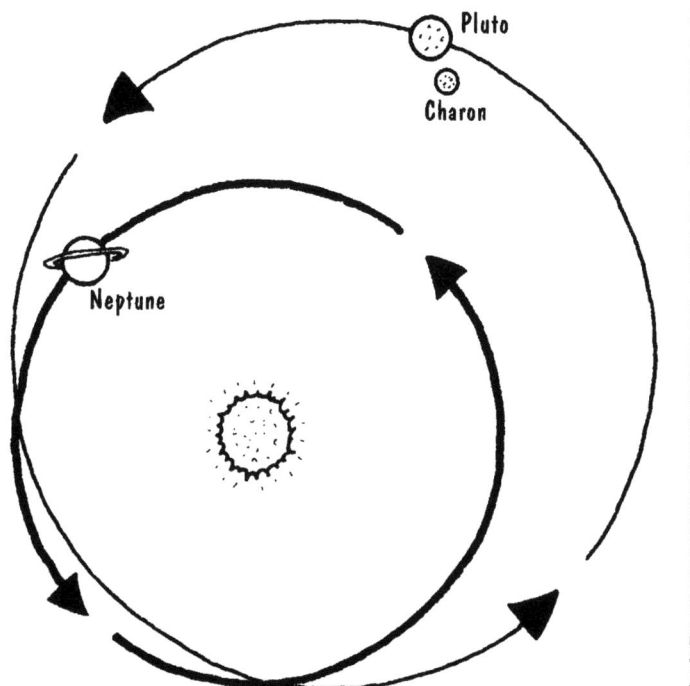

Pluto's irregular orbit sometimes causes the farthest planet in the solar system to be the second farthest. When Pluto crosses inside Neptune's path (as is the case until 1999), Neptune is the farthest planet in the solar system.

17°, while Neptune's is 1.8°. The two will never meet because they orbit the Sun at such different angles.

What is Pluto made of?

Pluto is very dense, so astronomers believe it is mostly rock (unlike its neighboring gas giants). It seems to be covered with ice, perhaps composed of methane and nitrogen. Bright and dark areas appear on the surface, and Pluto has polar ice caps.

Does Pluto have an atmosphere?

In 1988, when Pluto occulted—passed in front of—a star, astronomers were able to detect an atmosphere. If there were no atmosphere, the star would have blinked out like a light as soon as it was behind the planet's surface. But first, the star's light dimmed, as if passing behind

a film. That film was Pluto's atmosphere. It measures 180 miles (288 km) in depth, topping a dense surface haze some 28 miles (45 km) thick. The atmosphere may be composed of methane or methane and nitrogen.

What is Pluto's moon, Charon, like?

We know little about Pluto, and we know less about its only moon, Charon. Pluto's moon is about one-half the size of its host planet: 739 miles (1,182 km) in diameter. It orbits Pluto's equator at a height of 12,000 miles (19,200 km). Charon orbits Pluto in 6.4 days, which is the same as the planet's rotational period. This means that Pluto and Charon are gravitationally bound together, like two ends of a barbell.

When was the first rocket launched?

In 1926, Robert Goddard, a rocket engineer, fired the first rocket propelled by liquid fuel (solid fuel had already been discounted as not powerful enough to send anything into space). His rocket reached a velocity of 60 miles (100 km) per hour and height of 136 feet (12.5 m).

The first rocket did not reach orbit, but it was the precursor of all spacecraft. What distinguished it from other flying machines was that it was meant—one day—to shoot straight up into space.

How does a rocket work?

Rockets launch spacecraft. Without a good rocket, a satellite or space capsule isn't going anywhere. The basic workings of a rocket begin with a store of liquid fuel and one of liquid oxygen. The two liquids are funneled into a combustion chamber where they interact, causing the fuel to burn. The gas produced from the burning fuel is shot out of the rocket as exhaust—and thrust. As long as the fuel keeps burning and the gas keeps being released, the rocket will fly.

Launchers—rockets used to launch spacecraft—can have more than one stage. The stages ignite consecutively to give spacecraft the boost they need to break out of Earth's gravitational force. Once in orbit, or out in space, the rockets are discarded and the craft uses other means of power.

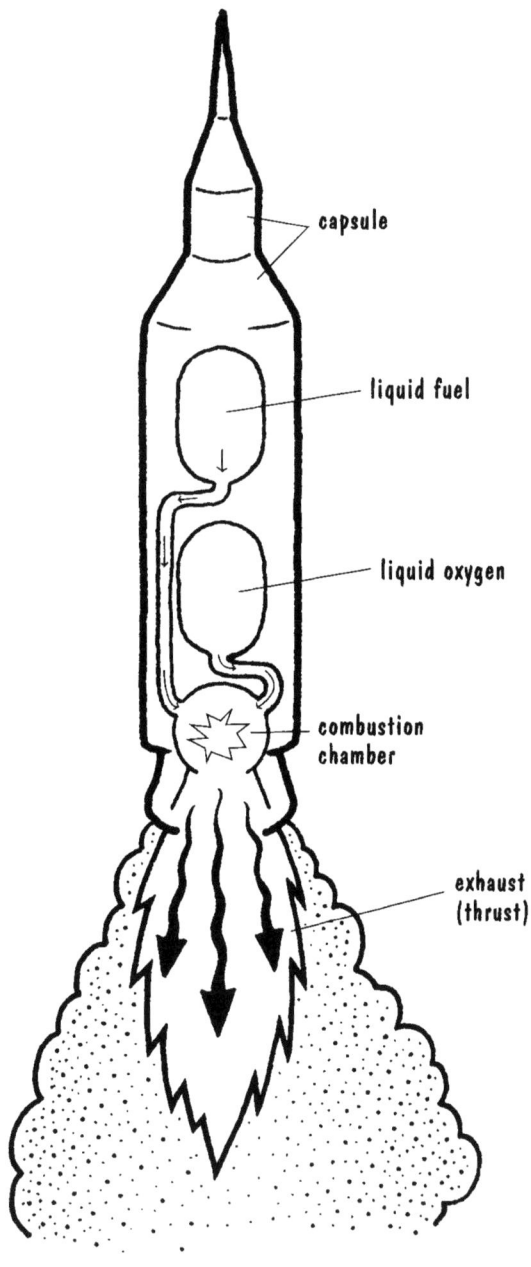

capsule

liquid fuel

liquid oxygen

combustion
chamber

exhaust
(thrust)

When liquid fuel and liquid oxygen combine, they combust, creating a
great amount of energy. The energy is thrust out of the bottom of the
rocket as exhaust, which propels the rocket until the fuel and oxygen
are used up. If the rocket has escaped Earth's gravitational force, the
capsule will stay in orbit until reverse thrusters are used for re-entry.

What was the space race?

In short, the space race was, and for some still is, a contest of power between Russia, formerly the Soviet Union (USSR), and the United States. It began with the USSR launching *Sputnik 1*. The march of history has limited, if not eliminated, the idea of a race, but it played a great part in the development of spacecraft and space launches.

When was the Sputnik launched?

On October 4, 1957, *Sputnik 1* was launched in the former Soviet Union, in Kazakhstan, near the town of Leninsk. This represented the first successful space launch. *Sputnik 1* was little more than a radio transmitter, but its 90-minute orbit of the Earth ushered in the space age.

The Space Race

In 1955, the United States and the Soviet Union (now Russia) both set up projects to send a satellite into space as soon as possible. Based on their development of missile technology during World War II, Werner von Braun led the U.S. effort and Valentin Petrovich Glushko and Sergei Pavlovich Korolov headed up the Soviet mission.

The prestige of being the first country to launch a satellite became a symbol of the political rivalry between the USSR and the United States. The race to space included the fight for the first satellites, the first manned flight, the first to the Moon, and the first space lab—not to mention the first and best communication and spy satellites.

One of the downfalls of the space race was the sacrifice of safety for speed. Another was that worthwhile scientific projects were delayed or abandoned in favor of the more spectacular race to put a human being on the Moon.

The Soviet *Sputnik 1*, a small radio satellite, beat the U.S. *Explorer 1* satellite into space by 121 days. The United States caught up, and even surpassed, its competitor in 1969, when it landed the first man on the Moon.

With the breakup of the Soviet Union in the 1980s and 1990s, and shifts in the priorities of both governments, the space race has taken on a different appearance. In the future, it is hoped that the race will look more like cooperation.

Was there more than one Sputnik?

The USSR launched two more Sputniks, one in 1957 and one in 1958. *Sputnik 2* carried a dog, named Laika, into orbit. She was the first living creature to travel in space. Laika did not seem to suffer from the launch, or from the weightlessness in orbit. The USSR, however, had not created a method of bringing her safely back to Earth. A week after the launch, Laika died due to lack of air. About 5 months later, *Sputnik 2* returned to Earth, and Laika was immortalized in history.

Sputnik 3 orbited for 691 days, studying micrometeorites, electromagnetic waves, and the Van Allen belts (radiation zones around Earth).

When did the United States launch its first satellite?

The news media called the Explorer's unsuccessful test run (1957) "Flopnik" and "Kaputnik."

The Soviet launch of *Sputnik* spurred the United States to get its first satellite, *Explorer 1*, into orbit. The National Advisory Committee on Aeronautics (NACA), the predecessor of the National Aeronautics and Space Administration (NASA), adopted a U.S. Navy plan called Vanguard to launch the country's first satellite. However, the satellite's test run, in December 1957, burned on the ground. *Explorer 1* was successfully launched into orbit around Earth on January 31, 1958.

What did the Explorer program do?

Sixty-five Explorer satellites—all unmanned—were launched from Earth between 1958 and 1984 (seven failed to launch successfully). They were all sent into space to collect data and conduct experiments on specific phenomena. The areas of study included radiation belts, magnetic fields, solar wind, electromagnetic rays, the ionosphere, and Halley's comet. In the aftermath of the *Challenger* disaster of 1986, the entire U.S. space program was modified, including the Explorer program. Further research of this kind would be conducted by "Small Explorers," smaller, less expensive satellites.

When did the United States begin its manned flight program?

In 1958, President Dwight D. Eisenhower established the National Aeronautics and Space Administration (NASA) to run the country's space programs. NASA contracted the McDonnell Aircraft Corporation (McDonnell-Douglas) to produce its design for a 9.6-foot (2.9-m) tall × 6.2-foot (1.88-m) wide capsule, just big enough for one person in a space suit. The name of the capsule design was Mercury; the specific capsules carried names such as *Liberty Bell*, *Freedom*, and *Friendship*. They were launched by various models of Saturn rockets.

How was the Mercury capsule tested?

In January 1961, the first Mercury was tested with a chimpanzee named Ham in a successful suborbital flight. Ham survived. About 4 months later, astronaut Alan B. Shepard also survived a successful suborbital flight.

When did a Mercury capsule first orbit Earth?

On September 13, 1961, a Mercury capsule was launched into orbit and, after one complete revolution, landed safely. On board was a simulation of an astronaut. Afterwards, a Mercury capsule successfully carried the chimpanzee Enos twice around Earth.

Who was the first American to orbit Earth?

Astronaut John Glenn Jr. was the first American to orbit Earth. His Mercury capsule, named *Friendship 7*, took off on February 20, 1962, and kept him in orbit for 5 hours. During reentry, NASA suspected that the capsule's heat shield (protection against the deadly heat of friction caused by falling through the atmosphere) might not remain in place. Glenn had to troubleshoot, but his landing was safe. All in all, six manned Mercury flights were completed in just over 1 year.

Who was the first person in space?

Not John Glenn! This honor went to Soviet cosmonaut Yuri Gagarin, on April 21, 1961—almost a year before

Vostok capsule

Glenn. The USSR reported a completely successful 1-hour and 48-minute orbit of the manned capsule *Vostok 1*. Later it was learned that trouble upon reentry caused the capsule's heat shield to grow so hot as to glow red. Gagarin had to eject himself and parachute to safety. This information, including the extent of Gagarin's injuries, was not released for some 30 years.

What were the missions of Vostok 2 through Vostok 6?

The USSR continued to use its Vostok capsule to send cosmonauts into orbit for increasingly long periods of time. Early in the 1960s, no one knew for sure whether people could survive space travel without serious side effects. Testing the limits of human endurance in space was an important process. Launched on August 6, 1961, *Vostok 2* carried cosmonaut Gherman Titov in orbit for more than one day (25 hours and 18 minutes).

Vostok 3 was launched on August 11, 1962. To the world's surprise, *Vostok 4* took off one day later. The two capsules intentionally came within 4 miles (7 km) of each other and communicated by radio. They stayed in orbit for 4 and 3 days, respectively. In June 1963, *Vostok 5* and *Vostok 6* were launched. Their plan was also to meet and establish radio contact in space. What most people didn't know at the time was that *Vostok 6* had a female cosmonaut, Valentina Tereshkova, at the controls. (The first American female astronaut in space was Sally Ride, aboard the space shuttle [the *Challenger*] some 20 years later.) The flights of *Vostok 5* and *Vostok 6* went smoothly, with *Vostok 5* setting a record for how long a person stayed in space: 5 days.

Spiders in Space

On July, 28, 1973, two spiders—Arabella and Anita—were launched toward *Skylab* and fame. Their mission was to spin webs in outer space. They boarded *Skylab* with three NASA astronauts. Arabella was put to work immediately. It took her about 2 days in space before she could spin normally. Anita was given a break for the first few days, after which she came out spinning perfectly normal webs.

What was the Gemini program?

The American Gemini spacecraft were the first to carry two people into space. NASA used them to test the effects on humans of longer and longer missions in space. *Gemini 7* broke the standing record for the duration of a space flight with a mission of 14 days, almost twice as long as a journey to the Moon would take.

Gemini also tested the reattachment—rendezvous and docking—abilities of the spacecraft and crews.

What was the first two-person flight?

NASA's *Gemini 3*, carrying Virgil Grissom and John Young, was launched on March 23, 1965. The test flight gave the astronauts a chance to try out maneuvers necessary to get to and from the Moon. Their flight lasted a short, but successful, 5 hours.

Virgil Grissom was the first person ever to fly into space twice: July 21, 1962 (Mercury), and March 23, 1965 (Gemini 3).

What was the purpose of Vokshod 1?

The USSR felt that they were lagging behind in the space race since the United States had sent two men—not just one—into space aboard *Gemini 3*. They converted the Vostok capsule, which had been designed for one cosmonaut (an astronaut in the Soviet, now Russian, space program) into a very cramped three-person spacecraft. On October 12, 1964, *Vokshod 1* carried three cosmonauts into a 1-day orbit around Earth.

Who was the first man to walk in space?

On March 18, 1965, Alexei Leonov stepped out into space from his *Vokshod 2* spacecraft, while his comrade Pavel Belyayev commanded the flight. Leonov wore a space suit and was connected to *Vokshod 2* by a tether and radio communication. His space walk was successful, but Leonov's space suit had expanded, and he was forced to reduce the air pressure inside it in order to fit back into the spacecraft. Upon entering Earth's atmosphere again, *Vokshod 2* suffered malfunctions and reentry had to be carried out manually. The cosmonauts could not rely on the automated reentry system but had to operate the spacecraft themselves—like parking a car when the engine and brakes aren't working right. It landed more than 600 miles (1,000 km) off course in a snow-covered forest. The cosmonauts got out, built a fire, and spent the night in the cold before rescue teams reached them.

What satellite was first to reach the Moon?

The first attempt by the USSR to crash-land a satellite on the Moon, in 1959, came close to succeeding. (No one as yet had the technology for a safe, soft landing.) The satellite, *Lunik 1* (also known as *Mechta* or *Luna*), flew by the Moon at a distance of only 3,300 miles (5,280 km). *Lunik 2*, launched on September 12, 1959, succeeded in crashing on the Moon. *Lunik 3* was launched into space the following month and sent back the first photographs of the far side of the Moon from orbit.

When did the first U.S. satellite reach the Moon?

The United States began its Pioneer program in 1958 under the auspices of the Department of Defense. Its purpose was to send a satellite into orbit around the Moon, but it never made it. NASA took over the program with the second attempted launch, on October 11, 1958, but had no better success. The closest they came was to send *Pioneer 4* some 36,000 miles (53,600 km) past the Moon. After three attempts, the Pioneer Moon program was abandoned.

NASA then developed the Ranger program. Haunted by mishap and failure, six Ranger satellites were launched before one was successful. *Ranger 7* triumphantly crashed into one of the Moon's mares, called the Sea of Clouds, on August 1, 1964.

What missions photographed the Moon?

During the final 13 minutes before it crashed into the Moon, *Ranger 7* sent back 4,316 photographs of the lunar surface. In 1965, two more Ranger satellites took pictures of the Moon before crashing, providing a total of more than 17,000 photographs. In February 1966, the USSR's *Luna 9* didn't crash, but landed safely on the Moon, and sent back panoramic photographs of its surroundings.

NASA's extensive Lunar Orbiter program sent five satellites into the Moon's orbit from August 1966 to August 1967. The Orbiter satellites were to photograph and map possible landing sights for a manned mission. They took pictures as close as 24 miles (40 km) from the surface with wide-angle and telephoto lenses. The first three missions were so successful that the last two were devoted to taking a photographic survey of the entire lunar surface. The Lunar Orbiter photographs are still some of the best images of the Moon.

What was the purpose of Surveyor 1?

No one had ever landed on the Moon, and in 1961, when NASA's Surveyor program began, some thought no one could. Controlling a safe landing on the Moon was critical to sending anyone up there. *Surveyor 1* was launched on May 30, 1966, and became the first U.S. spacecraft to make a controlled landing on the Moon. *Surveyor 1* touched down safely about 9 miles (15 km) from its programmed landing site.

What did Surveyor 7 accomplish?

Surveyor 7, launched on January 6, 1968, was the last satellite in NASA's Surveyor program. It carried equipment to test the Moon's soil. *Surveyor 7* scooped up lunar dust and rocks, and performed more than fifteen experiments on the soil, including tests to determine the amount of weight the surface could support.

Who was the first man to orbit the Moon?

There were three astronauts who could claim to be the first to orbit the Moon. On December 24, 1968, Frank Borman, William Anders, and James Lovell went into lunar orbit for 20 hours aboard *Apollo 8*. After their successful mission, the next step of the space program would be the one actually taken on the Moon.

When did the first man land on the Moon?

After ten Apollo test missions, both manned and unmanned, *Apollo 11* was launched on July 16, 1969. The astronauts on board were Commander Neil Armstrong,

Lunar Module Pilot Edwin "Buzz" Aldrin, and Command Module Pilot Michael Collins. On July 20, 1969, Armstrong and Aldrin landed the lunar module *Eagle* on the Moon's surface in the Sea of Tranquility. The landing was broadcast live across the United States. The astronauts planted an American flag and a plaque commemorating their achievement; spoke via telephone with Richard Nixon, then president of the United States; set up three experiments; and picked up samples of the lunar surface. They rendezvoused successfully with the command module and on July 24, 1969, returned safely to Earth.

How was the Apollo spacecraft constructed?

The 1960s saw a great debate among scientists and the U.S. government as to what kind of vehicle would work best for all three stages of the Apollo mission. The mission required a launch, a visit to the Moon, and a return to Earth. In the end, NASA decided to launch one spacecraft to orbit the Moon. Aboard was a lunar module, designed specifically to land on the moon, take off again, and hook up with the orbiting spacecraft. The lunar module could then be discarded, making reentry into Earth's atmosphere much easier and safer. The major problem with this plan was that the astronauts had to learn complex and difficult maneuvers for linking up spacecraft while in space. The Gemini program (1964–1966) and the early Apollo missions (1966–1969) took care of this with test runs.

What was the Apollo lunar module like?

The Apollo lunar module had two main functions: to land safely on the Moon and take off again. The module was shaped something like a four-legged, octagonal spider. With legs fully extended in landing position, it stood about 23 feet (7 m) tall and 31 feet (9.5 m) across. It weighed some 33,000 tons (15,000 kg), and held two astronauts, equipment for gathering lunar data and samples, a number of communication antennas, and two rocket engines: one for landing and one for taking off. The compartment for the crew was not luxurious. While landing, the astronauts stood up and wore harnesses for security. While on the Moon, the only place for them to sleep was in hammocks or on the floor.

What was the Apollo spacecraft like?

The orbiting Apollo spacecraft had two modules: the command module and the service module. The command module, where the three astronauts spent their time, measured 10 feet (3 m) × 12.5 feet (3.8 m). It had five windows and contained three couches for the astronauts; storage facilities; navigation, instrument, and control panels; space suits; food; and toiletries. The command module was linked to the lunar module by an air lock reached through a short tunnel. It was at this air lock that the astronauts in the lunar module had to disengage from and link back up with the spacecraft. The service module was about 13 feet (3.9 m) × 25 feet (7.5 m). It held rockets to reach lunar orbit and to begin reentry; equipment bays; scientific instruments; cameras; and electrical and life-support systems. There was an identical duplicate of every kind of life-support system in case of emergency.

What was the Apollo launch rocket like?

Saturn rockets, based on missiles developed by the U.S. Department of Defense, launched most of the Apollo missions. *Apollo 11*, which carried the first men to the Moon, used a Saturn 5 rocket. Saturn 5 rockets had three stages. Stage 1 was a rocket that measured 139 feet (42 m) high. It burned liquid oxygen and kerosene for just over 2 minutes to give the spacecraft its initial thrust and then fell away from the spacecraft. Stage 2 measured 82 feet (24.8 m) tall. It carried five engines that burned liquid oxygen and liquid hydrogen. Stage 2 worked for about 6 minutes before breaking away. Stage 3, which was 78 feet (23.7 m) tall, contained the engine and fuel to place the spacecraft into Earth's orbit and then, 90 minutes later, to send it out of orbit, toward the Moon. Stage 3 then disengaged and either went into orbit around the Sun or was sent to crash into the Moon.

What was the USSR's manned lunar program?

The USSR launched five missions (*Zond 4–8*) between 1968 and 1970, apparently as tests for a manned Moon landing, but the exact purpose of the missions has never been fully revealed to the scientific community.

The Soviet lunar program was dropped 3 years after U.S. astronauts Armstrong and Aldrin made it to the Moon and back.

The Soviet program seems to have depended on creating a new booster rocket. The N-booster, as it was known, used a total of forty-four rocket engines in five stages to send a two-man Soyuz spacecraft to orbit the Moon and a one-man lunar module to land. Rather than use a tunnel to reach the lunar module in space, a cosmonaut would have had to make a dangerous space walk to enter it. The Soyuz spacecraft never made it to the Moon, but it has been a very useful vehicle in Earth's orbit.

What was the Apollo–Soyuz mission?

In 1972, the United States and USSR agreed to meet in space. Three years later, *Soyuz 19* and an Apollo capsule, the last to be used in the space program, docked and for 2 days exchanged crews and good will. In preparation for this historic, albeit mostly symbolic, mission, many problems had to be overcome. Among them, the Apollo and Soyuz programs used different docking mechanisms and air (Apollo used pure oxygen under low pressure; Soyuz used oxygen and nitrogen under higher pressure). To solve the problems, the two countries developed a docking module in which the air quality could be altered slowly enough to avoid physical distress. The docking went off without a hitch and both Apollo and Soyuz returned home triumphantly.

Why are space suits necessary?

Space suits are required because body fluids would boil under the natural pressure in space. Even pilots of high-flying aircraft need pressurized suits, and NASA

Tragedies in Space

Traveling in space is dangerous. No possibility of life exists beyond the support functions brought from Earth. Getting off and back onto Earth requires the use of highly volatile and dangerous materials. Space travelers are face-to-face not only with the laws of physics, but also their own mortality.

The first fatal accident occurred on January 27, 1967, relatively early in the history of manned flights. U.S. astronauts Virgil Grissom, Edward White, and Roger Chaffee boarded *Apollo 1* for a routine countdown test. The test was not considered dangerous because the rocket was not fueled; however, poor insulation of electrical wires apparently started a fire in the capsule, which was filled with pure oxygen. The astronauts died of smoke inhalation before the capsule was engulfed in flames.

The Soviet space program experienced its first fatality on April 23, 1967, when a Soyuz capsule's parachute failed to operate properly. The capsule crashed, killing cosmonaut Vladimir Komarov.

A successful mission aboard the Soviet space station *Salyut 1* turned into tragedy as the *Soyuz 11* spacecraft carrying three cosmonauts back to Earth malfunctioned. A valve intended to let air in just prior to touchdown sprang open early on in the journey home. The capsule's air was instantly sucked out into the vacuum of space, and Georgi Dobrovolsky, Vladislav Volkov, and Victor Patseyev were suffocated.

The fatal explosion of the space shuttle *Challenger* on January 28, 1986, was witnessed by millions of adults and children, who watched the launch because of its historic value. Christa MacAuliffe, a schoolteacher, and Gregory Jarvis, a Hughes Aircraft employee, had been chosen to be the first civilians to go into space. Seconds after launch, a fire ignited and the shuttle exploded almost instantly. Along with MacAuliffe and Jarvis, Dick Scobee, Mike Smith, Ellison Onizuka, Ron McNair, and Judy Resnik perished in the disaster.

The first man in space, Yuri Gagarin, died on March 27, 1968, in an aircraft accident while training for a Soyuz mission. Our gratitude to these brave men and women, and their families and friends, should never diminish.

NASA's technical term for space suit is extravehicular mobility unit (EMU).

developed space suits for the Mercury astronauts from those originally worn by U.S. Navy jet pilots.

What were Gemini space suits like?

When astronauts began walking in space, their suits had to be further altered to give more mobility and comfort while providing more protection from micrometeorites and accidental rips and tears. The Gemini space suits were airtight casings enclosed by a layer of woven fishnet fabric that prevented ballooning when the suit was pressurized. A layer of felt and seven layers of insulation lay under a nylon outer covering for protection against temperature changes. Life support was provided by the spacecraft through a tube connected to the midsection of the suit.

Were there special space suits for lunar landings?

Experience showed that overheating was a problem in Gemini space suits. The Apollo space suits had a layer of fabric made of tubing through which cool liquid flowed. A layer of linen provided some comfort, and the use of rubber, nylon, and aluminum ensured protection. Life support had to be mobile, so a backpack with oxygen, cool water, and a power source was developed. Apollo's space helmets were attached to the suits, allowing more freedom of head movement without danger of leaking at the neck connection. Boots were worn over the layers of the suit and had a special protective coating on the outside.

What do space shuttle astronauts wear?

Space suits on the space shuttles are required only for launch and landing. There are so many astronauts now, space suits are no longer individually tailored to each one. The different parts—arms, legs, torso, etc.—come in different sizes and need only be attached to each other for a customized fit. A layer of tubing filled with a cool liquid is closest to the skin. The outer suit is made of many layers, including dacron, thermal nylon, urethane, and aluminum (mylar). The boots are already attached to the pants. The

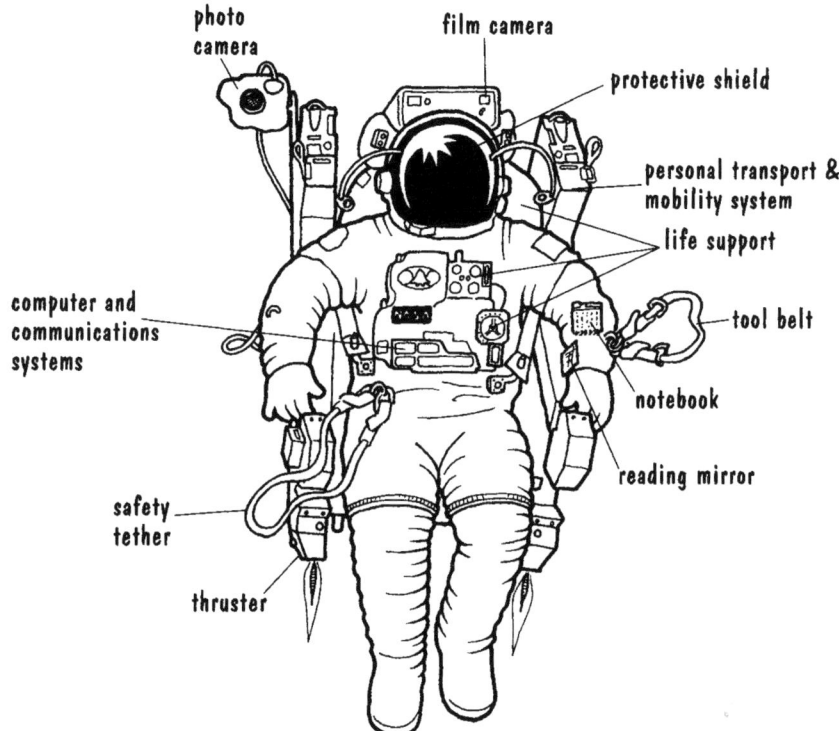

photo
camera

film camera

protective shield

personal transport &
mobility system

life support

computer and
communications
systems

tool belt

notebook

safety
tether

reading mirror

thruster

Space suits have come a long way since Soviet cosmonauts flew in nothing but their underwear. Constantly updated designs and technology allow astronauts to explore space, conduct experiments, and record data without being tied to the base ship.

torso is made of inflexible fiberglass, and the helmet is attached. This section is put on like a suit of armor, over the head. The life-support systems and a radio are contained in a built-in backpack. Space shuttle space suits are orange.

Do cosmonauts wear space suits?

They do now, at least during takeoff, landing, and docking. Originally, space suits were not required, and some cosmonauts flew in their underwear. But on June 29, 1971, when the three cosmonauts in *Soyuz 11* undocked from the space station *Salyut 1*, an air release valve suddenly opened. Without the life-support systems of a space suit, the men suffocated. From then on, space suits have been mandatory at all critical phases of space journeys. They are one-piece suits that pressurize and cool, and carry life-support instrumentation in the pants legs.

What is a space station?

A **space station** is an orbiting satellite that is meant to accommodate a crew of astronauts over an extended period of time—weeks or even months.

What was the first space station?

On April 19, 1971, the USSR launched the first manned space station, *Salyut 1*, into orbit around Earth. The station consisted of four compartments, and was meant to house three crew members for up to 4 weeks. The entry compartment had the docking equipment for the spacecraft that would carry cosmonauts to and from the station. The work compartments—cylinders approximately 10 feet (2.9 m) around × 13 feet (3.9 m) long and 14 feet (4.15 m) × 13.5 feet (4.1 m)—held the controls, instruments, a treadmill, a table, and sanitation fixtures. The fourth compartment stored the propulsion system. The first five Salyut stations mostly failed to work properly. *Salyut 6* and *Salyut 7* were modified and were home to many successful long-term and record-breaking missions between 1977 and 1986. In 1986, the USSR's *Mir* space station took over.

When was the U.S.'s space station Skylab launched?

The first U.S. version of a space station, *Skylab*, was launched on May 14, 1973. The astronauts on the first mission had to spend a great deal of time repairing the station, which had seriously malfunctioned from the time it took off. They were able to fix it and complete their planned experiments within 28 days. Two more missions used—and had to repair—*Skylab* successfully. Major studies involved observations of Earth, solar flares, and the comet Kohoutek, plus research into the medical effects of long-term space travel.

Skylab

What is the space shuttle?

Originally, the **space shuttle** was meant to be a transport system to and from a space station. Due to financial cutbacks and shifts in priority at NASA, the space station never materialized, but the space shuttle did. The space shuttle became an orbiting laboratory as well a reusable spacecraft for transportation into space. A major key to its success is its flexibility in taking on different kinds of missions, while being reusable. It can perform maintenance and repairs on satellites as well as scientific research. The shuttle can carry up to eight astronauts—ten if necessary. It is designed to stay in orbit for up to 10 days, though 5 days is the typical length of a mission. While the space shuttle has had its disasters, it seems to be remarkably successful.

Does Russia have a space shuttle?

The USSR developed and built the space shuttle *Buran* in the late 1970s and 1980s. *Buran* looks very much like the U.S. space shuttle. The USSR space shuttle took off on its maiden voyage in November 1988. Unlike the U.S. space shuttle, which takes off under its own power, *Buran* was rocketed into orbit and then released. *Buran's* unmanned orbit, lasting 3 hours and 25 minutes, was a successful test of its maneuverability and landing. Political changes accompanying the dissolution of the USSR and the re-creation of Russia put a hold on further *Buran* missions.

What other countries have space programs?

Most industrialized countries probably have some kind of space program. This is not to say that they all put people into space. Most concentrate on launching communications and/or surveillance satellites. Manned space flight is becoming more and more a cooperative international effort. For example, the *Freedom* space station, announced in President Ronald Reagan's 1984 State of the Union address, involves the efforts of the United States, Japan, Canada, and the European Space Agency (whose member states include the United Kingdom, Denmark, Norway, Sweden, Finland, Belgium, the Netherlands,

Switzerland, Austria, Germany, France, Italy, and Spain). China's first satellite, *Tungfang hung*, was launched on April 24, 1970. Details of the Chinese manned space flight program are kept secret by the Chinese government, but photographs of astronauts in training have been released. China has also discussed possible cooperative missions with Russia and the United States.

India, Israel, and Japan all have national programs to launch and maintain satellites and to join other countries, particularly the United States, in sending their citizens into space.

What is the Spacelab?

A joint space mission between NASA and the European Space Agency (ESA), *Spacelab* was first launched in November 1983. *Spacelab* is not a spacecraft in and of itself. It consists of varying modules that travel attached to the space shuttle for the purposes of conducting specific research. Each module is 9 feet (2.7 m) by 19 feet (4 m) and can be used as a work space or can carry instruments such as telescopes. Other units, called pallets, can be attached for cargo that does not need to be pressurized. The Spacelab depends on the shuttle for living space and life support, but carries everything else in pressurized modules or unpressurized pallets.

What is the Freedom space station?

Once the race to the Moon was over, attention could be refocused on long-range missions. The idea of a permanently manned, international space station came into favor. Funding was short and NASA's first priority became the space shuttle, but in 1984, President Reagan announced in his inaugural speech that such a station would be next on the agenda. The superstation *Freedom* was born.

As the plans now stand, the space station *Freedom* is to be built (with international cooperation, particularly between the United States, European nations, Japan, and Canada) in space before 1999. The estimated cost is at least $25 billion. Ultimately, a crew of four will always be on board, but each crew member will stay about 90 days.

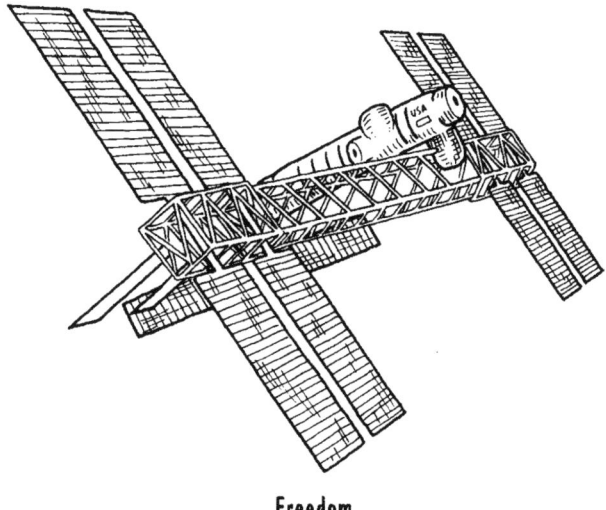

Freedom

There are many designs for the proposed international space station *Freedom*. Preferred designs would allow additional structures to link permanently; would have an independent lab station that could work undisturbed by the coming and going of shuttle craft carrying passengers and equipment; and would carry a special "lifeboat" capsule for evacuation.

Transportation of the crew, supplies, equipment, and building materials will be via the space shuttle. An "assured crew return vehicle," probably similar to an Apollo capsule, will be a part of *Freedom*'s permanent structure; its purpose will be to evacuate the crew in case of an emergency.

Have any spacecraft studied the Sun?

NASA developed a number of Orbital Solar Observatories (OSO), which were launched between 1962 and 1975. Their purpose was to observe the Sun's ultraviolet, gamma, and X rays throughout an 11-year sunspot cycle. From 1973 to 1974, a special Apollo Telescope Mount (ATM) was attached to *Skylab* for observation of the Sun. The successor to the OSO program was called the Solar Maximum Mission (SMM), which studied the Sun during the climax of sunspot activity. The SMM was launched in 1980, repaired by a shuttle crew in 1984, and continued to operate until 1989.

Solar observations have also been carried out by France, Japan, and the USSR. Special attention has been given to the phenomenon of solar wind by NASA, the ESA, and the USSR.

What do probes do?

Probes are unmanned spacecraft fitted with instruments to gather and transmit data and/or images from space. Because they are self-sufficient, they can be sent where no person could survive: into orbit around the Sun, to the other planets, or even out beyond the solar system. The downside of unmanned probes is that malfunctions need to be taken care of from Earth (or the space shuttle), which could be millions or billions of miles away. Much of the information we have about the Sun and the planets came from space probes such as Pioneer, Mariner, and Voyager.

Why do we keep sending new probes to the same planets?

Advances in understanding and technology—as well as the failure of some probes to perform their tasks—make it important to send probes time and again to the same planet. We don't know what we will find when we receive information from a distant probe. Every probe sent to Jupiter, for example, raises more questions than existed before. *Voyager 1* discovered ten more moons orbiting Jupiter than we had seen from Earth. To find out more about those satellites, further probes are necessary. The first probes were only able to fly by planets, catching a mere glimpse of them. When scientists figured out how to intentionally put a probe in orbit around another planet, we were able to see entire planets.

Nevertheless, there is only so much any one probe can accomplish in a mission. Successive missions are needed to carry out further research. And consider a probe sent to the Sun. If it passes Venus and Mercury on its way, we don't want to miss an opportunity to receive new information by not turning it on as it goes by, even if other probes have been there before.

What planets did the Mariner probes visit?

Mariner 2, the first successful planetary probe launch, was sent into Earth's orbit on August 27, 1962. From there a rocket fired it on a 4-month journey to Venus. On November 28, 1965, *Mariner 4* came within 540 miles (870 km) of Mars and sent back the first pictures of the planet's surface. *Mariner 6* and *Mariner 7* (1969) both took detailed pictures of approximately 10 percent of the Martian surface, but missed some of the most interesting geological features later discovered by *Mariner 9*. *Mariner 9* (1971) was the first satellite to enter into orbit around Mars. After waiting out a Martian dust storm, *Mariner 9* sent back pictures of the entire planet. *Mariner 10*, the final Mariner probe, had a dual mission. On February 5, 1974, it flew by Venus and transmitted more than 3,000 pictures of the planet's surface. It then went on to Mercury. *Mariner 10* photographed approximately 40 percent of Mercury's surface before entering into orbit around the Sun. In this orbit, the probe was able to pass by Mercury twice more: over the south pole and over the dark side of the planet. The Mariner program was hailed as a great success.

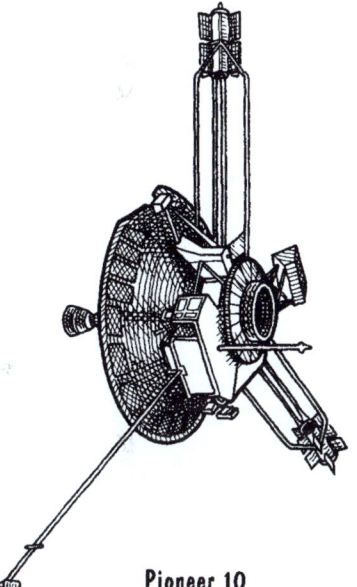

Pioneer 10

What planets did the Pioneer probes go to?

Pioneer 10 (1972–1973) was designed to send radio signals back to Earth from Jupiter. It took the probe 21 months to reach the gas giant. While it had no cameras, it was also able to scan part of Jupiter's surface and send back clearer images than had ever been taken from Earth. *Pioneer 11* (1973–1974) used Jupiter's gravitational force to launch itself toward Saturn. It sent back the first photographs of that planet. Both *Pioneer 10* and *Pioneer 11* went on to gather data from beyond the solar system. It is hoped that *Pioneer 10* will relay data into the twenty-first century; however, due to technical troubles, *Pioneer 11* is not expected to last that long.

Both **Pioneer 10** *and* **Pioneer 11** *carry bronze plaques aboard, giving directions on how to reach Earth for anyone out there who may find them.*

When did Voyager probes go to the gas giants?

Voyager 2 was launched first, on August 20, 1977, but *Voyager 1*, launched on September 5, 1977, beat it to Jupiter. *Voyager 1* made its closest pass on March 5, 1979, and collected detailed information about the planet and its moons. *Voyager 2* got to Jupiter in July 1979.

In November 1980, *Voyager 1* transmitted data and photographs of Saturn to Earth. It went on to study Saturn's largest moon, Titan. Flying by Titan meant that *Voyager 1* could not make it to Uranus. *Voyager 2* reached Saturn in August 1981, and flew on, passing Uranus on January 24, 1986. Three and a half years later, it approached Neptune and the planet's moon Triton. After completing their planetary investigations, both Voyager probes continued to send back information on their unguided journeys into deep space.

When did Viking probes visit Mars?

Mariner probes had already orbited Mars, but the Viking program was designed specifically to land on the planet in search of—among other things—life. *Viking 1* went into orbit around Mars on June 19, 1976. NASA planned to send a module to land on the surface on Independence Day, to celebrate the U.S. bicentennial, but complications delayed the landing until July 20. *Viking 2* landed on September 3 that same year. Both probes were outfitted with biological experiments to determine whether there was any sign of life on Mars. For friends of Martians, the results were disappointing. The Viking probes did not discover any biological evidence of life on that planet, but they studied the soil, weather, and atmosphere, and sent back over 42,000 photographs.

What is Mars Global Surveyor's mission?

Launched on November 6, 1996, NASA's Mars *Global Surveyor* probe is designed primarily to study past and present climate patterns, carry out studies of geology and natural resources to determine the possibility of Mars supporting manned missions; and, of course, to look for life. Many astronomers expect that any vital signs on the planet will point to life that existed hundreds of thousands of years ago rather than any contemporary beings.

The discovery, early in 1996, of traces of life potential on a 600,000-year-old meteorite from Mars hastened the Mars *Global Surveyor* project. This is the first part of a decade-long series of missions to Mars, called the Mars Exploration Program. *Global Surveyor* will conduct mapping operations, monitor weather, and collect data of surface features.

What probes did the USSR launch to Venus?

The Venera program focused on landing a probe on Venus. The first probes sent back data and images from within the planet's atmosphere before being burned up by the incredible temperatures or crushed by the monumental atmospheric pressure. *Venera 7* touched down on July 22, 1972, and relayed the first data ever gathered by a probe actually on the surface of another planet (although it did so for only for 23 minutes). The first surface images ever taken of Venus were transmitted by *Venera 9* and *Venera 10* in October 1975.

What was the USSR's Mars program?

The USSR's Mars program (the probes were named for the planet) had more than its fair share of misfortune, including failed launches, unsuccessful attempts to leave Earth's orbit, completely missing Mars, and even death. (Scientists set out to investigate the failed launch of an early probe; it exploded, killing most of the team.) Out of seven spacecraft, only one actually touched down. *Mars 3* reached the surface through a terrible dust storm on December 2, 1971. It immediately began to send images to Earth, but shut down after 20 seconds.

Where did the USSR's Phobos probes go?

The Phobos probes (1988–1989) were intended to erase the bad memories of the largely disastrous Mars program of the 1970s. Designed to orbit Mars and land on the planet's moon Phobos, the two probes were launched in July 1988. An incorrect command sent to *Phobos 1* shut the probe down and it was lost. *Phobos 2* took 6 months to reach Mars. It orbited Mars for several weeks, and then adjusted its orbit to include Phobos. As *Phobos 2* prepared to release its two landing modules onto the moon's surface, contact was permanently lost. The Phobos program was not a complete disaster, since images and data from *Phobos 2*'s orbit around Mars reached Earth, but it was a disappointment.

What did the USSR probe Vega achieve?

The USSR's Martian program did not meet expectations, whereas its 1985 Vega probes to Venus and Halley's comet were unmitigated successes. By 1985, international relations had eased to the point where the USSR, the United States, Europe, Brazil, and Australia all shared information on this venture. *Vega 1* and *Vega 2* were launched in December 1985. Both sent landing modules to Venus's surface in June and released balloons to monitor the atmosphere and weather. Then the probes reoriented themselves and journeyed toward Halley's comet's orbit. *Vega 1* was the first probe to reach the comet, passing it at a distance of 5,000 miles (8,000 km). Both probes gathered data on the comet and sent the information back to be used by the European probe *Giotto* in its mission to Halley's comet.

What probes were sent to Halley's comet?

An international fleet of probes were launched to intercept the orbit of Halley's comet in 1986. The Soviet *Vega 1* probe was the first to reach its destination, on March 6, coming within 5,000 miles (8,000 km) of the comet's nucleus. *Vega 2* arrived to take photos from a distance of 13,000 miles (21,000 km) 3 days later. *Vega 1* transmitted data that helped to ensure the success of the ESA's *Giotto* probe, which reached the comet 7 days later. On March 8, the Japanese probe *Suisei* passed Halley's comet at a distance of 91,000 miles (146,000 km) in order to get a long view. Also from Japan, the probe *Sakigake* was sent to study the comet's tail. *Giotto*'s mission was to fly directly into the comet's coma and photograph it for as long as possible before it collided head-on with the nucleus. The probe transmitted its live television footage almost to the point of impact. Instead of a collision, however, the

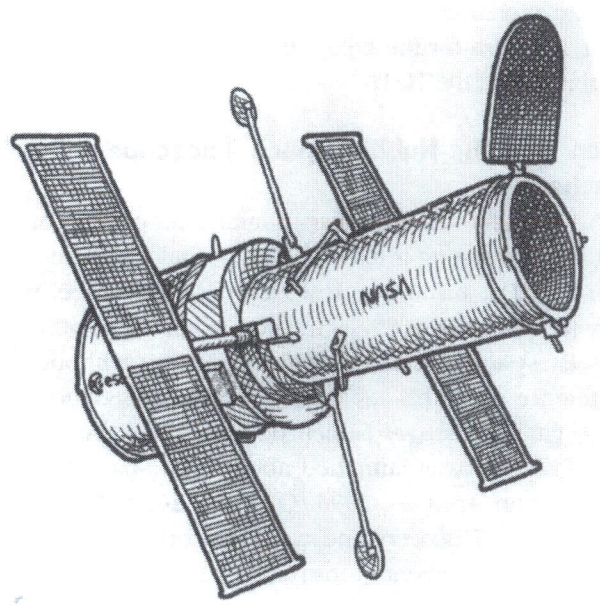

Hubble Space Telescope

probe was knocked out of the comet's path by a grain of dust weighing only 3 one-hundredths of an ounce (1 g). An hour or so later, *Giotto* again began sending data as it flew past the comet.

What is the Hubble Space Telescope?

Since telescopes were first used by Galileo in the early seventeenth century, astronomers have dreamed of placing them where Earth's atmosphere would not get in the way of viewing the universe. The Hubble Space Telescope (HST) fulfills that dream. The HST, a reflecting telescope, is not the largest telescope made on Earth. Its amazing clarity comes from its position beyond the distorting interference of Earth's atmosphere. The HST has a primary mirror that is 7.9 feet (2.4 m) in diameter. In addition to the telescope unit itself, the HST has two cameras, two spectrometers (to break up the components of light), and a photometer (to measure brightness). Its control system for locating stars uses gyroscopes and special star-tracking and sensor devices. The HST is NASA's baby, but an international effort went into its construction and out-fitting. In return for the help, other countries get observation time using the HST.

When was the Hubble Space Telescope launched?

NASA spent some 30 years thinking about, designing, creating, and testing a telescope that would be launched into orbit. The result, the Hubble Space Telescope, was ready for launch in 1985. Its mission would be to observe the solar system and the galaxies beyond it without the interference of Earth's atmosphere. Early in 1986, however, the fatal *Challenger* launch postponed all NASA projects. The HST was launched aboard the space shuttle *Discovery* on April 24, 1990. On April 26, 1990, it was released from *Discovery* and went into orbit. All maintenance and replacement of instruments is to be carried out by the space shuttles.

Was there trouble with the Hubble Space Telescope?

Fortunately, NASA made plans for repairing the HST throughout its projected 15-year orbit. Two months after the HST's launch, it was discovered that the primary mirror had not been ground properly (among other problems). The telescope could not be focused.

While this was a major embarrassment, the dangerous and complex repair mission was a coup. The space shuttle *Endeavor* was launched in December 1993. Its crew captured the HST, fixed it, and released it successfully. The images and data returned since have more than outweighed the early difficulties, promising that the HST will be remembered for its scientific achievements rather than its flaws.

What is the next major NASA mission?

Plans change all the time, due to budgetary and governmental constraints, but the next planned space spectacular is an extended trip around Saturn and a landing on its moon Titan. The mission is a collaborative effort between the ESA and NASA. The spacecraft *Cassini,* as it is called, has been partly developed from Mariner, Viking, and Voyager equipment. The landing probe, named *Huygens*, will come from the ESA. *Cassini* is hoped to reach Saturn a few years into the twenty-first century. After a month-long orbit, the spacecraft will fly by Titan in order to drop the *Huygens* probe onto the moon's surface. (Little is known about Titan's surface, and there is some concern that *Huygens* will soon sink in a sea of liquid methane.) *Cassini* will then attempt to use the satellite's gravity to boost it toward Saturn's other moons. If successful, *Cassini* will spend some 4 years bouncing off various moons' gravity fields, studying the satellites as well as Saturn's rings.

It is likely that the first person to set foot on Mars has already been born.

Will there ever be off-world settlements?

The idea of colonies of humans on the Moon or Mars lies not only between the pages of science fiction paperbacks. NASA has been planning a lunar base since the 1960s. Investment in the space shuttle program drew attention away from this goal, but interest has been revived. In 1991, veteran astronauts described some likely scenarios. Perhaps a lunar base would be used for training missions to Mars. Or the focus may be on scientific study of the Moon itself, which would call for a different kind of base. A scientific community could be up and running by the year 2015. If the idea is to set up a permanent colony on the Moon, a self-sufficient community of some six astronauts could be started by 2010.

Selected Space Exploration Programs

Name	Country	Dates	Achievements	Selected astro-/cosmonauts
Sputnik	USSR	1957–1958	First satellite	
Explorer	U.S.	1958–1984	Science experiments	
Pioneer	U.S.	1958	Moon research	
Lunik	USSR	1959	Moon landing	
Vostok	USSR	1961–1963	First manned flight	Valery Byskovsky, Yuri Gagarin, Adrian Nikolayaev, Pavel Popovitch, Valentina Tereshkova, Gherman Titov
Mercury	U.S.	1961–1963	Americans in space	Malcolm Scott Carpenter, L. Gordon Cooper, John Glenn, Virgil Grissom, Walter Schirra, Alan Shepard
Venera	USSR	1961–1983	Venus research	
Ranger	U.S.	1961–1965	Moon landings	
Mariner	U.S.	1962–1974	Mercury, Venus, Mars	
OSO	U.S.	1962	Solar study	
Mars	USSR	1962–1971	Mars research	
Vokshod	USSR	1964–1965	Three-man space flight	Pavel Belyayev, Konstantin Feoktistov, Vladimir Komarov, Alexei Leonov, Boris Yegorov
Gemini	U.S.	1964–1966	Lunar flight tests	Edwin Aldrin, Neil Armstrong, Frank Borman, Eugene Cernan, Michael Collins, Charles Conrad, L. Gordon Cooper, Virgil Grissom, James Lovell, James McDivitt, Walter Schirra, David Scott, Thomas Stafford, Edward White, John Young
Luna	USSR	1966	Moon photography	
Lunar Orbiter	U.S.	1966–1967	Camera in lunar orbit	

Selected Space Exploration Programs

Name	Country	Dates	Achievements	Selected astro-/cosmonauts
Surveyor	U.S.	1966–1968	Lunar robot	
Apollo	U.S.	1966–1975	Manned Moon landing	Edwin Aldrin, William Anders, Neil Armstrong, Alan Bean, Frank Borman, Eugene Cernan, Michael Collins, Charles Conrad, Walter Cunningham, Charles Duke, Don Eisle, Richard Gordon, Fred Haise, James Irwin, James Lovell, Edgar Mitchell, Stuart Roosa, Walter Schirra, Harrison Schmitt, Russell Schweickart, David Scott, Thomas Stafford, Jack Swigert, Alfred Worden, John Young
Soyuz	USSR	1967–1986	Space station; transportation	Vladimir Dzanibekov, Georgi Grechko, Alexei Gubarev, Pyotr Klimuk, Vladimir Remek, Yuri Romanenko, Victor Savinykh, Svetlana Savitskaya, Vladimir Shatalov, Vitaly Stevastyanov, Vladimir Vasyutin, Vladimir Volkhov
Salyut	USSR	1971–1986	Manned space stations	
Skylab	U.S.	1973–1974	First U.S. space station	Alan Bean, Gerald Carr, Charles Conrad, Owen Garriott, Edward Gibson, Joseph Kerwin, Jack Lousma, William Pogue, Paul Weitz
ATM	U.S.	1973–1974	Solar study	
Apollo-Soyuz	U.S./USSR	1975	International venture	Vance Brand, Valeri Kubasov, Alexei Leonov, Donald Slayton, Thomas Stafford

Selected Space Exploration Programs

Name	Country	Dates	Achievements	Selected astro-/cosmonauts
Voyager	U.S.	1977–1986	Gas giants studied	
SMM	U.S.	1980–1989	Solar study	
Space shuttle	U.S.	1981–?	Reusable manned craft	Patrick Baudry, Roberta Bondar, Vance Brand, Robert Crippen, Reinhart Furrer, Jake Garn, Marc Garneau, Edward Gibson, Jack Lousma, Ken Mattingly, Ernst Messerschmid, Sally Ride, Dick Scobee, Kathy Sullivan, Richard Truly, Charles Walker, Paul Weitz, John Young
Spacelab	U.S./ESA*	1983	Reusable space laboratory	Ulf Merbold
Vega	USSR	1985	Atmospheric study of Venus; photograph Halley's comet	
Mir	USSR	1986–?	Space station	Victor Afanasyev, Alexander Alexandrov, Anatoli Artsebarsky, Totar Aubakirov, Alexsandr Baladin, Jean-Loup Chretien, Mohammed Faris, Klaus-Dietrich Flade, Sergei Krikalev, Leonid Kzim, Alexander Laveikin, Anatoli Levchenko, Vladimir Liakhov, Gennadi Manakov, Musa Manorov, A. Mohmand, Varery Poliakov, Yurii Romanchenko, Victor Savinyth, Alexsandr Serebrov, Alexander Solovyev, Vladimir Solovyey, Gennadi Strekalov, Vladimir Titov, Hans Vietiboeck, Alexsandr Vitorenko, Alexsandr Volkov

Selected Space Exploration Programs

Name	Country	Dates	Achievements	Selected astro-/cosmonauts
Giotto	ESA*	1986	Photograph coma of Halley's comet	
Suisei	Japan	1986	Photograph Halley's comet from a distance	
Buran	USSR	1988	Space shuttle	
Phobos	USSR	1988	Photograph and study geophysiology of Mars	
Galileo	U.S.	1992–?	Photograph and study atmosphere of Jupiter	
Cassini	U.S. /ESA*	1996	First detailed study of Saturn, Titan	

*ESA: European Space Agency

GLOSSARY

A

absolute magnitude   how bright a star would be in comparison to other stars if all stars were seen at a distance of 10 parsecs from Earth

active galaxies   colliding galaxies that produce jet streams of matter and energy

aperture   the diameter of the lens or primary mirror of an optical telescope

aphelion   the point in a celestial body's orbit when it is farthest from the Sun

apparent magnitude   how bright a star appears in comparison to other stars when seen from Earth

asteroid   celestial matter that may not necessarily be left over from the planets' formation (as is a planetesimal); asteroids may be parts of planets that were knocked into space by a collision

asteroid belt   the ring of asteroids that orbits the Sun between the orbits of Mars and Jupiter

astronomical unit (AU)   a measure used to describe distance within the solar system; equal to 93 million miles

auroras   displays of light that occur as solar wind interacts with Earth's electro-magnetic fields

B

baryonic matter   all known matter in the universe; made from photons and neutrons

big bang theory   popular theory of the beginning of the universe that states that all existence began with a vast surge (not really an explosion) of energy and matter from which all else evolved

big crunch   a nickname for the closed universe model, designating the opposite of the big bang

black dwarf   dead stars of carbon cores and virtually no remaining helium shell

black hole   a vast celestial mass contracted into a relatively tiny space causing increased gravitational force capable of attracting all nearby objects and matter, including electromagnetic radiation

C

cannibal galaxies   galaxies that consume smaller galaxies in their proximity

Cassegrain telescope   a reflecting telescope with a curved, concave secondary mirror that allows for greater flexibility in enlarging and focusing incoming light

Cassini division   a gap in Saturn's ring system between the two most prominent rings, rings A and B

celestial bodies   natural objects in space, such as planets, galaxies, comets, and stars; also called heavenly bodies

celestial globe   the spherical map of the night sky as seen from Earth

celestial horizon   the 180° encircling line where the sky meets Earth from a stargazer's point of view

celestial sphere   the dome of lights surrounding Earth

circumpolar stars   stars that neither rise nor set, but encircle a polestar above a stargazer's celestial horizon

closed universe model   a theory that states that the universe will ultimately contract in upon itself through gravitational force

comet   a frozen mass of rocky debris from space in orbit around the Sun

constellations   groups of stars seen from Earth and identified by name, such as Leo, the Big Dipper, and Orion

cosmology   study of the evolution and structure of the universe

crater   the depression caused by the impact of a meteorite

D

dark matter   undiscovered material that theoretically makes up some 90 percent of all matter in the universe

declination (dec)   the imaginary vertical lines on the celestial sphere used with right ascension to locate position of celestial objects; corresponds to latitude lines on Earth

E

ecliptic   the path the Sun appears to take around Earth (in fact, Earth revolves around the Sun)

electromagnetic spectrum   the array of energy radiation detected in the universe, separated by frequency and wavelength into gamma rays, X rays, ultraviolet rays, light rays, infrared rays, and radio waves

elliptical galaxy   a galaxy in the shape of an ellipsis (an oval anywhere from almost a circle to almost a flat pancake)

elongation   the greatest distance of a planet's orbital ellipsis east or west of the Sun

epoch   the specific moment in time depicted on a celestial globe

equatorial bulge   a spreading out of mass at a celestial body's equator due to the force of the object's rapid rotation

exosphere   the space beyond Earth's atmosphere; outer space

F

favorable opposition   when a superior planet (to Earth) is at its perihelion while in alignment with Earth and the Sun

flat universe model   a theory that the rate of expansion of the universe will even out the rate of gravitational contraction until the universe reaches a point of rest

focal distance   the distance incoming light travels within an optical telescope before reaching the focal point, where it becomes focused for viewing; also known as focal length

focal point   the spot within a refracting telescope where incoming light is focused

G

galactic clusters   groups of galaxies held in formation by mutual gravitational force

galactic year   the time it takes our solar system to rotate around the nucleus of the Milky Way, about 250 million years

galaxy   a mass of stars held together by gravitational force; the most prominent units that make up the universe

gamma rays   deadly radiation of energy at the highest wavelength and frequency; they occur during thermonuclear fusion and are detectable in supernovae

gas giants   Jupiter, Saturn, Uranus, and Neptune, so called because they are primarily made of gas and they are very large planets

geocentric model   a theory of the organization of the solar system that places Earth at its center

globular clusters   densely packed groups of stars appearing in the spherical region around a galaxy, called the galactic halo

granules   undulating waves of gas on the Sun's surface

gravity   the force of attraction exerted by an object with mass

H

heliocentric model   a theory of the organization of the solar system that places the Sun at its center

Hertzsprung-Russell diagram   a chart that plots stars according to luminosity, absolute magnitude, and temperature

I

incline   see orbital tilt

inferior conjunction   when an inferior planet is in alignment (syzygy) between the Sun and Earth

inferior planet   any planet that orbits the Sun at a closer distance, e.g., Mercury and Venus are Earth's only inferior planets

inner planets   those planets on the inner side (closer to the Sun) of the asteroid belt: Mercury, Venus, Earth, and Mars

interstellar medium   the gas and dust that occupies space between stars

ionosphere   a layer of Earth's atmosphere carrying electrically charged molecules; it overlaps the mesosphere and thermosphere

irregular galaxy   a galaxy with a shape that is neither spiral nor elliptical

K

Kelvin (K) scale   a system of measuring extreme temperatures used in astronomy; 0°K = −460°F (−273°C); 98.6°F = 310°K (37°C)

Kuiper Belt   a band of asteroids, planetisimals, and other celestial debris beyond Neptune's orbit; comets may originate there

L

latitude   imaginary vertical lines on Earth used together with longitudes to help locate position of terrestrial objects

light rays   energy emission of the wavelength and frequency that is detectable by the human eye

light-year (lt-yr)   the time it takes light to travel in 1 year; a measure used to describe distance in outer space; equal to 5.9 trillion miles (9.29 trillion km)

limb   the outer edge of the Sun or any celestial disk

Local Group   the name of the galactic cluster to which the Milky Way belongs

Local Supercluster   the name of the supercluster to which the Local Group (including the Milky Way) belongs

longitude   imaginary horizontal lines on Earth used together with latitudes to help locate position of terrestrial objects

luminosity   the measure of a star's energy output, similar to the measure of a lightbulb—only much greater

lunar eclipse   the effect of syzygy when the Sun, Earth, and Moon line up with Earth in the middle, thereby casting the Moon in its shadow

M

magnetic field   the natural magnetic force of a planet or other celestial object

magnetic poles   the positively and negatively charged focal points of a magnetic field; on Earth, the magnetic north and south poles

magnetosphere   a large tear-shaped field of electromagnetic particles around Earth

main sequence stars   the term used for mature stars; stars that fall along the diagonal midsection on the Hertzsprung-Russell diagram from hottest and brightest to coolest and faintest

mesosphere   the third layer of atmosphere from Earth's surface

meteor   any type of celestial matter in the solar system; most frequently used to describe debris falling within an atmosphere, but burning up before impact

meteor shower   the display of lights that occurs as Earth travels through the path of a comet's orbit

meteorites   meteors that make contact (collide) with the surface of a celestial object planet's surface

minor planets   the asteroids within the asteroid belt between Mars and Jupiter

N

nebula   a dense area, or cloud, of interstellar medium (gas and dust between stars)

neutrinos   subatomic particles that are emitted in large numbers during thermonuclear fusion

neutron star   theoretically the core of a star that has exploded in a supernova; made of neutrons (atomic particles with no electrical charge)

neutrons   atomic particles with no electrical charge and slight mass found in all atomic nuclei, with the exception of hydrogen; one of the building blocks of all known matter

nonbaryonic matter   theoretical matter not based on the building blocks of photons and neutrons

nova   the bright flare as a white dwarf in a binary star system is joined to its neighboring star

nucleus   this word has many meanings, including the center of a cell, galaxy, or atom, and the rocky core of a comet

O

objective lens   the lens at the opening of an optical telescope that gathers light

occultation   when a celestial object crosses in front of, and obscures, another celestial object

omega   in cosmology, the term for the unknown, but critical, amount of mass that theoretically will determine the outcome of the universe

Oort Cloud   an outlying area of the solar system from which comets are thought to originate

open clusters   loose groups of stars appearing in a galaxy's nucleus and spiral arms

open universe model   a theory that states that the universe will continue to expand forever

orbital plane   the imaginary flat surface (plane) along which a planet, or other celestial body, orbits the Sun

orbital tilt   the angle of a planet's orbit plane in reference to Earth's orbital plane; also known as incline

outer planets   planets whose orbits lie beyond the asteroid belt: Jupiter, Saturn, Uranus, Neptune, and Pluto

P

parallax   the degree of angle between the two lines of a triangle arising from the baseline; in astronomy, used to determine the distance of stars

parsec (pc)   a measure of extremely great distance within the universe, equal to 3.26 light-years or 19 trillion miles (30.4 trillion km)

perihelion   the point in a celestial body's orbit when it is closest to the Sun

photons   atomic particles that make up electromagnetic radiation; they have no mass, but are conveyors of energy in both particle and wave form; building blocks of all known matter

photosphere   the layer of the Sun that we see as its surface

planetary nebula   the cloud of an old-age star that has thrown off its outer shell of hydrogen

planetisimals   original matter from the Sun's explosion into a mature star that did not become part of a full-fledged planet

polestar   the star designated as the North Star, that identifies the location of the celestial north pole

precession   the circular movement of an axis

primary mirror   the mirror in a reflecting telescope off which incoming light is first reflected

prime focus   the spot within a reflecting telescope where incoming light is focused

protoplanet   the mass of dust, gases, and debris ejected during the explosion of a new star, which are coalescing to become a planet

protostar   an early stage of a star just prior to gaining enough mass to spark thermonuclear fusion, thereby becoming a full-fledged star

pulsars   high-density celestial objects that emit regular bursts of radiation (mostly radio waves), which many scientists believe are, in fact, neutron stars

Q

quasars   the most distant observable objects in the universe, thought to be the centers of highly active, young galaxies

R

radio dishes   the name given to instruments that gather radio waves as a telescope collects light rays

radio waves   relatively long wavelength and slow frequency energy emission useful in detecting cooler objects in space, such as nebula

rays (crater) visible streaks emanating from a crater, created by material that was thrown out beyond the crater's edge upon a meteorite's impact

red dwarfs main sequence stars at the cooler, fainter end of the Hertzsprung-Russell diagram

red giants (also super giants) cool, but bright and luminous nonmain-sequence stars

reflecting telescope an optical telescope that uses mirrors to gather and enlarge light

refracting telescope an optical telescope that uses ground glass lenses to gather and enlarge light

retrograde in opposite direction from the norm

right ascension (RA) the imaginary horizontal lines on the celestial sphere used with declination to locate the position of celestial objects; corresponds to longitude lines on Earth

S

satellite a natural or manufactured object in space that orbits a host planet

secondary mirror a mirror in a reflecting telescope off which incoming light bounces toward an eyepiece, through which the incoming light can be viewed

Seyfert galaxies highly active galaxies that emit 100 times the electromagnetic radiation of ordinary galaxies

sidereal time the system of keeping time based on a day of 23 hours, 56 minutes, and 4 seconds, the time it takes Earth to complete one rotation

solar eclipse the obscuring of the Sun from the view of Earth when a full or new Moon lines up directly between the star and planet

solar system the organization of celestial bodies orbiting the Sun and the space they inhabit

solar time the system of keeping time based on a 24-hour day, the time it takes the Sun to reappear in the same spot at high noon

space shuttle a reusable spacecraft originally designed to travel between Earth and an orbiting spacecraft

space station a permanent or semi-permanent orbiting satellite intended to house laboratories, equipment, and crews in space for extended periods of time

spectral classes categories of stars based on their temperatures; from hottest to coldest: O B A F G K M (remembered by the phrase **Oh Be A Fine Guy [Gal], Kiss Me**)

spiral galaxy a type of galaxy with a round nucleus and arms that spiral out like a pinwheel

star clusters groups of stars held in relative formation by mutual gravitational force

steady state theory the theory that the universe is balanced by the creation of new mass to replace loss of mass, thereby escaping the fate of both the closed- and open-universe models

stratosphere the second layer of atmosphere from Earth's surface

sunspots shadows on the Sun's surface indicating magnetic disturbances

superclusters a group of galactic clusters held together by mutual gravitational force

superior conjunction when the Sun is in direct alignment (syzygy) between an inferior planet and Earth

superior planet   any planet that orbits the Sun at a farther distance, e.g., Mars, Jupiter, Saturn, Uranus, Neptune, and Pluto are Earth's superior planets

supernova   the explosion of an old-age star with a carbon core hot enough to spark carbon fusion

syzygy   the direct alignment of three or more celestial bodies, frequently used in reference to the Sun, Moon, and Earth during an eclipse

T

terrestrial planets   Mercury, Venus, Earth, Mars, and Pluto; so called because they are primarily made of rocky material similar to Earth

thermonuclear fusion   the process by which elements react with heat to form other elements, e.g., 4 hydrogen atoms combine and interact to form 1 atom of helium; the basic source of a star's energy

thermosphere   the fourth, and final, layer of atmosphere from Earth's surface

total solar eclipse   a solar eclipse during which the Moon completely hides the Sun from view on Earth

trace chemicals   chemicals that appear in very small amounts, or traces

transit   when a smaller celestial object crosses in front of a larger one

troposphere   the layer of atmosphere nearest Earth's surface

U

ultraviolet rays   energy emission with wavelength and frequency greater than visible light, but less than X rays; evidence of extreme mass and temperature, and, sometimes, celestial activity, such as the explosion of a star

unfavorable opposition   when a superior planet (to Earth) is at its aphelion while in alignment with the Sun and Earth

V

vernal equinox   in astronomy, the base latitude (0^h) from which right ascension is counted (up to 24^h)

voids   regions of space between superclusters that apparently contain no galaxies, but may hold the theoretical dark matter of the universe

W

wavelength   in radiation astronomy, the time between the peak of one wave of energy and the next

white dwarfs   hot, but faint stars not on the main sequence; old-age stars; made mostly of a carbon core and a helium shell

X

X rays   second fastest radiation emission; evidence of highly compact and fast-moving objects in space

Z

zenith   in astronomy, the point above a stargazer's head where north-south and east-west arcs cross

BIBLIOGRAPHY

Barrow, John D. *The Origin of the Universe*. New York: Basic Books, 1994.

Brass, Charles O. *The Essentials of Astronomy*. Piscataway, NJ: Research and Education Association, 1995.

Caes, Charles J. *Studies in Starlight: Understanding Our Universe*. Blue Ridge Summit, PA: Tab Books, 1988.

Cohen, Nathan. *Gravity's Lens: Views of the New Cosmology*. New York: John Wiley & Sons, 1988.

Davies, J. K. *Space Exploration*. Edinburgh: Chambers, 1992.

Denecke, Edward J. *Let's Review: Earth Science*. Hauppauge, NY: Barron's Educational Series, 1995.

Dolan, Terrance. *Probing Deep Space*. New York: Chelsea House, 1993.

Frazier, Kendrick, and eds. of Time-Life Books. *Solar System: Planet Earth*. Alexandria, VA: Time-Life Books, 1985.

Hamburg, Michael. *Astronomy Made Simple*. New York: Doubleday, 1993.

Jastrow, Robert. *Red Giants and White Dwarfs*. New York: W. W. Norton, 1990.

Lauber, Patricia. *Journey to the Planets*. New York: Crown, 1993.

Lightman, Alan. *Time for the Stars: Astronomy in the 1990s*. New York: Viking, 1992.

Moche, Daniel L. *Astronomy: A Self-Teaching Guide*. New York: John Wiley & Sons, 1993, 1994.

Moore, Patrick. *Atronomers' Stars*. New York: W. W. Norton, 1987.

————. *Atlas of the Universe*. N.p.: Rand McNally, 1994.

Morris, Richard. *Cosmic Questions*. New York: John Wiley & Sons, 1993.

The New American Desk Encyclopedia. 3rd ed. New York: Meridian, 1994.

The Random House Dictionary of the English Language. unabridged ed. New York: Random House, 1983.

Reidy, David, and Ken Wallace. *The Solar System: A Practical Guide*. North Sydney, Australia: Allen & Unwin, 1991.

Ridpath, Ian. *Star Tales*. New York: Universe Books, 1988.

Silk, Joseph. *The Big Bang*. rev. ed. New York: W. H. Freeman, 1989.

Tyson, Neil de Grasse. *Universe Down to Earth*. New York: Columbia University Press, 1994.

Uvarov, E. B., and Alan Isaacs. *The Penguin Dictionary of Science*. 7th ed. London: Penguin, 1993.

VanCleave, Janice Pratt. *Astronomy for Every Kid*. New York: John Wiley & Sons, 1991.

THE
NEW YORK PUBLIC LIBRARY'S
RECOMMENDED READING LIST

Bonnet, Robert L., and G. Daniel Keen. *Space and Astronomy: 49 Science Fair Projects*. Blue Ridge Summit, PA: TAB Books, 1992.

Bova, Ben. *Welcome to Moonbase*. New York: Ballantine Books, 1987.

Branley, Franklyn M. *Venus: Magellan Explores Our Twin Planet*. New York: HarperCollins, 1994.

Butterfield, Moira. *Space*. New York: Dorling-Kindersley, 1994.

Couper, Heather, and Nigel Henbest. *How the Universe Works*. Pleasantville, NY: Reader's Digest, 1994.

Darling, David J. *The Galaxies: Cities of Stars*. Minneapolis: Dillon Press, 1985.

Gallant, Roy A. *The Planets: Exploring the Solar System*. New York: Four Winds Press, 1989.

Gutsch, William A. *The Search for Extraterrestrial Life*. New York: Crown Publishers, Inc., 1991.

Hatchett, Clint. *Discover Planetwatch*. New York: Hyperion, 1993.

Kelch, Joseph W. *Small Worlds: Exploring the 60 Moons of Our Solar System*. Englewood Cliffs, NJ: Julian Messner, 1990.

Lampton, Christopher. *Astronomy*. New York: Franklin Watts, 1987

Lauber, Patricia *Journey to the Planets*. New York: Crown Publishers, 1990.

————. *Seeing Earth From Space*. New York: Orchard Books, 1990.

Miller, Ron, and William K. Hartman. *The Grand Tour: rev. ed.* New York: Workman Publishing, 1993.

Millspaugh, Ben. *Aviation and Space Projects*. Blue Ridge Summit, PA: TAB Books, 1992.

Moskin, Marietta D. *Sky Dragons and Flaming Swords*. New York: Walker and Company, 1985.

Sullivan, George. *The Day We Walked on the Moon*. New York: Scholastic, 1990.

Verba, Joan Marie. *Voyager, Exploring the Outer Planets*. Minneapolis: Lerner Publications Company, 1991.

Vogt, Gregory L. *The Hubble Space Telescope*. Brookfield, CT: Millbrook Press, 1992.

————. *Solar System*. New York: 21st Century Books, 1995.

Watters, Thomas R. *Planets: A Smithsonian Guide*. New York: Macmillan, 1995.

INDEX

Printed and bound by CPI Group (UK) Ltd, Croydon, CR0 4YY

08/12/2025

14786550-0001